PATRIARCH.

for him

eau de dad

time for a *new* spice:
PATRIARCH.
a new fragrance for him

A lusty combination of pine,
fresh cut grass & cedar chips

available at all fine department stores

 PATRIARCH.

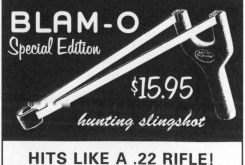
On the Cover:

MARVIN WARRINGTON

This month's cover model hails from Scaggsville, just north of Baltimore, and has been a loving husband to his wife Marlene for over forty years. They are the proud parents of six: Darlene, Michelle, Dawn, Tammy, Rhonda, and Marvin Jr.

Marvin's favorite pastime is wood crafting in his meticulously organized basement workshop. "Organization is the key to happiness," says Warrington. "A place for everything, and everything in its place." When not tinkering around in his workshop, Marvin can be found scouring eBay for rare Slim Whitman, Leonard Nimoy, and Telly Savalas vinyl. As of this issue's publication, his collection stands at over 75 albums, including the extremely rare *Telly Savalas Christmas Album*.

Marvin has been an avid *Dad Magazine* reader for over twenty years, his first exposure being a Father's Day present from his eldest daughter, Darlene. After his wife secretly contacted our offices, Marvin got the surprise of his life when we called him to be our next cover model. "I'd been eyeing-up those dads on the cover of *Dad Magazine* for years, never dreaming that one day it would be me."

A big "thank you" to Marvin for taking time out of his busy schedule, to Marlene for making us aware of her husband, and to all the Warringtons for their hospitality in allowing us to invade their home to shoot in the basement workshop.

HEY, GOOD LOOKIN'!
A NOTE ABOUT THE REDESIGN

Eagle-eyed readers will notice something a *little* different about this issue. Yes, *Dad Magazine* has gotten a "makeover," but don't you worry—none of these new-fangled fonts and fancy-schmancy flourishes will overpower the quality paternal content you know and love.[1] While we at *Dad Mag* have always prided ourselves on simplicity, thrift, and do-it-yourselfedness, the fact of the matter is that it was time to change, and one of our kids knows this guy who does good design work on the computer for pretty cheap.[2] We know you'll miss the clip-art illustrations and hand-stapled spines,[3] but, as longtime subscribers will note, this isn't the first time we've made an upgrade (like when the mimeograph-ink shortage of '99 prompted a switch to dot-matrix printing, for example). We hope that our readers will embrace all the new dood-dads (get it, doo-DADS) and remember that it's what's on the inside that counts.[4] And speaking of insides, check out that full-color section in the middle! Boy, was that thing a pain in the neck to wrangle. You would not BELIEVE what those clowns think they can charge you for color ink! Man.

Happy reading!

The *Dad Magazine* Staff

NOTES FROM THE CREATIVE DIRECTOR:

[1] Hey guys, we tried! We wanted to give the magazine a *real* makeover, but they insisted on using most of the same typefaces, photographers, and ad designers that they've always used. We *did* manage to sneak in some up-to-date elements to help keep things a *bit* current. I hope you enjoy!

[2] We are a respectable, professional studio, and we don't even know their kids! They came to us for our expertise, not because we are cheap—though we did give them a price break because they're a great bunch of guys, though I'm sure you know from past issues how thrifty they are.

[3] Why on earth would anyone miss that?

[4] I'm sure you guys will adapt!

VOLUME 100   ISSUE 1   JUNE 2016

PUBLISHED BY
Famlé Nast

EDITOR-IN-CHIEF:
ART PARKER

MANAGING EDITOR:
John Frangelico

DESIGN DIRECTOR:
Paul Kepple

SENIOR EDITOR:
Floyd McAllister

EDITOR-AT-LARGE:
Harry Froelich

DEPUTY EDITOR:
Skylerr Lincoln

NON-CONTACT SPORTS EDITOR:
Larry Sheehan

SPORTS AND FITNESS EDITOR:
Gerald Wen

STAFF WRITERS:
Clint Hardlam, Oliver Gibson
Gary Gottileb, Kirk Neale
Maurice Tunstall
Dave "Mr. Cleo" Clemens

— ART —

SENIOR DESIGNER: Max Vandenberg
DESIGNER: Caleb Heisey
PHOTOGRAPHER: Michael Reali
PHOTO RESEARCHER: Dexter Fishpaw
PRODUCTION ARTIST: George Demharter

— COPY —

SENIOR COPY EDITOR: Rodger McMartin
COPY EDITOR: Darren Plainfield

DAD MAGAZINE
A SUBSIDIARY OF
FAMLÉ NAST
· PUBLICATIONS ·
EST. 1979

For editorial and advertising inquiries, write to Famlé Nast
Publications, P.O. Box 1479 Talisman Lane, New York, NY 10010,
or call our offices at 212-555-5554. For subscriptions and address
changes write to Dad Magazine, P.O. Box 487, Newark, NJ 07114,
or call our toll free number (800) 999-9997

Library of Congress Cataloging in Publication Number: 2015946942

ISBN: 978-1-59474-864-6

Designed by
HEADCASE DESIGN:
Paul Kepple, Max Vandenberg, Caleb Heisey
www.headcasedesign.com

Crossword puzzle on page 126 by Aimee Lucido
Production management by John J. McGurk

QUIRK BOOKS
215 Church Street · Philadelphia, PA 19106
quirkbooks.com

THANKS TO OUR ALL DAD MODELS:

*Dave Berson, Rob Brothers, Scott Carpenter, Rick Chillot, Israel Del Rio,
John Ford, Anuj Gupta, Gary Horner, Otto Kuchar, David Low, Keith Marlowe,
David Mercuris, Jeff Podraza, Mike Rogalski, David Thornburgh, Mark Tucker,
Jeff Weir, Dwayne Wharton, Luke Wolff*

PHOTOGRAPHY: **MICHAEL REALI:** workshop background on front cover and pg. 2; pg. 72 ties; pg. 73: book and fannypack; pg. 79 August 2006; back cover / **FLICKR:** pgs. 6-7 Art Parker courtesy of Rifqi Dahlgren rifqisphoto.com, John Frangelico courtesy of Ged Carroll, Floyd Mcallister courtesy of Andy Tyler, Harry Froelich courtesy of Gerald Wen courtesy of Dennis Yang, Skylerr Lincoln courtesy of Trevor Leyenhorst; pg. 12 courtesy of Ashley Campbell; pg. 16 Jackalope courtesy of CGP Grey; pg. 17 dad with tattoos courtesy of Tom Good, dad with saw courtesy of WoodleyWonderworks, dad with fish courtesy of David Jakes; pg. 90 fratboy courtesy of NVM; pg. 95 courtesy of Katy Warner; pg. 99 Pat M. courtesy of Cristina Valencia, Dave R. courtesy of cheriejoyful, Skip courtesy of Boris Thaser; pg. 105 courtesy of Jim Fischer / **ISTOCK:** front cover and pg. 2 by fatihhoca, inside front cover by IPG Gutenberg UK Ltd; pg. 1 couple by Pali Rao, bottle by ronen; pg. 6 Clint Hardlam by monkey-businessimages; pg. 8 old couple by Neyya, Jacuzzi by Radekk; pg. 9 by Szeyuen; pg. 10 man on phone by Aldo Murillo, screwdriver by Chimpinski, donut by Matt Jeacock, WD-40 by Lebazele, peace sign by DRB Images LLC, ; pg.11 duck by rusm, bowler by Susan Chiang, man in chair by kazoka30, angry man by Steve Luker; pg. 13 reel-to-reel by narvikk, cd by 7io, floppy disc by Token Photo; pg. 18 golf cart by artticnew; pg. 21 DIAMANDPHOTO; pg. 28 "Weird Uncles" cover by Cameron Whitman; pg. 29 by CREATISTA; pg. 30 recliner by Atilla ALTUN; pg. 33 by Juanmonino; pg. 34; pg. 35 by Diane Labombarbe; pg. 39 ranch dressing by Juanmonino; pg. 40 farmer by Nicolas McComber; pg.54 by Michael Krinke; pg.56 hippy-scraggle by Flamingo Photography and Debbi Smirnoff, lunatic by sutulastock, over-dye by stockyimages; pg.57 au naturale by stockyimages, dali by selimaksan, imperial and chevron by ozgurdonmaz, Santa by Petar Chernaev, chin curtain by XiXinXing; pg. 61 backdrop by jpgfactory, Rico by Jason Doly, Marvin by by_nicholas; pg. 62-3 backdrop by evirgen; pg. 64 golf backdrop by boggy22, bike backdrop by Maxfocus, bike by SL-Photo; pg. 65 backdrop by FOTOGRAFIA INC.; pg. 66-7 backdrop by maghakan, pheasants by Jason Lugo, Albert by Ljupco, bear by Philip Cacka; pg. 68-9 backdrop by Falombini; pg. 72 bolo tie by Jason Lugo, bandanas by Jani Bryson, cigars by bibikoff, top pipe by igorr1, bottom pipe by StockPhotosArt, drill by manley099, newspaper by DNY59, gloves by miklosuz, slippers by Don Nichols; pg. 73 belt buckle by skodonnell, suspenders by WestLight, ballcap by jojoe7333, top glasses by Kashtan, watch by kimeveruss, goggles by Tempura, fur cap by Don Nichols, fishing hat by DNY59, step counter by Hayes Photography; pg. 74 by Christine Glade; pg.75 by Lobsterclaws; pg. 79 August 1988 by thawornnurak, May 1996 by sandocir, January 2000 by tap10, March 2002 by sturti, July 2010 by Curtis Creative, December 2014 by PonyWang; pg. 89 by digger1948; pg. 90 grass by DonNichols, banana by harmpeti, dog by Eric Isselée; pg.96 ice chest by Don Nichols, toolbox by teptong; pg. 97 bike by talevr, grill by gemenacom; pg. 99 Les W. by delihayat; pg. 104 junk equipment by smiltena; pg. 102 palm pilot by CostinT; pg. 103 carphone by LockieCurrie, vcr by PaZo; pg. 109 by DNY59; pg. 114 jazz illustration by taolmor; pg. 115 pencil by yuriz, eraser by jangeltun, sharpener by AD Photo; pg. 118 by JazzIRT; pg. 119 by saknakorn; pg. 125 glue gun by Denis Dryashkin; pg. 128 man in chair by Susan Chiang; inside back cover by Susan Chiang / © **DREAMSTIME.COM:** pg. 10 baseball; pg. 11 seahorse; pg. 20; pg. 22 tweakbait, quake-n-fish, snagthrusts, hurdy-gurdy-man, bangarang; pg. 28 "Dad for Kids," "Matronly Monthly;" pg. 30 bowling ball; pg. 37 bottle cap; pg. 39; pg. 40 potato chips; pg. 41 wrap, cow; pg. 56: comb-over; pg. 58; pg. 72 cigar cutter, knife, Allen keys; pg. 73 round glasses, sunglasses, comb; pg. 79 March 1989; pg. 96 car rear; pg. 103 typewriter, pg. 104 blackberrry and computer; pager; pg. 112 / **SHUTTERSTOCK:** pg. 41 bloody mary by Kittibowornphatnon; pg. 61 Louis by Gualtiero Boffi; pg. 83 by Ljupco Smokovski; pg. 91 by Menzl Guenter

CONTENTS

EVERY MONTH

6   Contributors
7   Letter from the "Dad"itor
8   Letters from Our Readers

9   Dad of the Month
10 The Informed Father
12 Ask a Dad

15 Faux "Pa"s
16 Look What I Found
17 Dadshots

FEATURE ARTICLES

78
100 YEARS OF *DAD MAGAZINE* IN COVERS
TAKE A TOUR OF DADS PAST

80
OUR DAD CENTURY
The story of the past
100 years of
Dad Magazine

82
HERO DAD GETS QUIET TIME
The inspiring story of one
man who finally found some
peace and quiet

84
A LACK OF VISION
A crime wave is putting
dads across the country at
risk. So why isn't the FBI
taking a stand?

87
THE FATHER OF DANGER
Read the tantalizing tale of a
dad on the run in this excerpt
from the master of Paternal
Fiction Jim Hopper's new book

SPORTS + FITNESS

20 Lately, Every Sport Has
    Been Ruined!
22 Tackle Box Guide
24 Your Best Hunting Weekend
    Itinerary
26 Point/Counterpoint:
    How Good Is the Sun?
30 Health Hacks:
    Trick Your Body into Being Healthy
32 The Heart of the Matter
33 Father Figure

FOOD + DRINK

37 Make Beer in Your Basement:
    The Dad Way!
39 Op-Ed:
    Look at This New Pizza Stone!
40 Dad Mag Trend Watch:
    Food
43 Tips on Waitstaff Interaction
44 Point/Counterpoint:
    What Is the Spice of Life?
46 My First Grill:
    A Personal Story
48 The Only Five Recipes You Need
    to Know
    (Seriously, Don't Learn Any More)

FASHION + GROOMING

56 A Hairy Situation
59 How To Talk to Your Son about
    Growing a Beard
60 Dad Rags:
    Special Fashion Section
72 Bits and Pieces

HOME + LIFE

90   Get These Things Off Your Lawn
91   Gary's Garden Corner
93   What's Going On with Your
     Neighbor's Yard?
95   Op-Ed:
     *These Smoke Detectors Are Too
     Damn Sensitive, If You Ask Me*
96   How to Pack Your Trunk
98   Makin' Great Time:
     America's Favorite Routes
100 Rear-View Danglers
101 Car Maintenance:
     *Why You Should Never Go to
     the Mechanic*
102 Dad Mag Tech Watch
105 Emoticons "Ur" Daughter
     Will Love ;-)
106 A Dad-Tastic Future, Today!
     The Latest in Dad Innovations

MONEY + WORK

110 Show Your Love through
     Stock Tips
112 How to Buy Shoes on eBay:
     Some Pointers
113 Hotel Handouts:
     What to Nab on Your Next Stay

JUST FOR FUN

116 Come to Think of It…
     Washington Was a Lousy General
118 My Favorite Movie:
     One Man's Search to Remember
119 Where to "Catch" *Field of Dreams*
     on TV This Month
120 Quiz:
     *What Completely Random Thing
     Should You Be Surprisingly
     Knowledgeable About?*
121 Gimme a Sign:
     Horoscopes Just for Dads
122 Dad Mag Crossword
123 Dad-Libs:
     Calling Your Kids Made Easy

CONTRIBUTORS

ART PARKER (or "Arts and Farts," as we like to call him) is the Editor in Chief of *Dad Magazine*. After graduating from Rutgers University, he began his career selling his soul copywriting for a popular men's outerwear catalog. Once he became a dad, however, he knew he had to realize his dream of fostering a place where dads could come together and exchange a "fatherload" of ideas, and so he began contributing to *Dad Magazine*. The rest is history! Parker lives in a real fixer-upper on Rhode Island's Narragansett Bay. In his spare time, he enjoys clamming, looking at trees, and playing Frisbee with his dogs. You know, the ones the kids promised they would take care of, but he's not surprised. You know what? Let's not do this here.

<from: John Frangelico "peanutbutter-andgelico@hotmail.com"
to: me
subj: DAD MAGAZINE BIO!!!
/

JOHN FRANGELICO is Managing Editor at *Dad Magazine*. After graduating from ucla, frangelico was the arts editor at the alt-weekly the venice beach weirdo, and later worked as a buyer for several prominent los angeles art galleries. he lives on the beach with his wife, and enjoys spending time with his grown kids, hosting dinner parties, listening to opera, and seeing movies in 70mm.
/
sent from john's iphone
/>

FLOYD MCALLISTER, *Dad Magazine*'s Senior Editor, earned a Mechanical Engineering degree from Clark Atlanta University and makes a living designing HVAC for hospitals. A lifelong tinkerer, he spends his weekends working on old cars, electronics, or just organizing his workshop to relax. He's always game to watch old sci-fi movies or a NOVA special on VHS with his wife and three kids.

CLINT HARDLAM writes for *Dad Magazine*. He lives in Racine, Wisconsin, and is very busy, thank you.

HARRY FROELICH doesn't really know how to write one of these doo-dads! Well I'm the Editor at Large of *Dad Magazine* and a proud Buckeye from Columbus, OH. My great-grandpa founded the magazine, too, I should probably say that. I'd been working as a floor manager in a sporting goods store but always had a passion for the written word, and my husband said, "Hey Harr-ball, why dontcha just write for them!" and I've been helpin' out ever since. Otherwise I enjoy kicking back, hanging out with friends, watching the game, and lake fishing with the kiddos.

GERALD WEN is *Dad Magazine*'s Sports and Fitness Editor. Gerald hails from San Jose, CA, and the weather's been so great, he hasn't wanted to leave! He's been a health en-thusiast ever since signing up for his high school's fitness team, where he eventually made captain (Go Fightin' Scholars!) He still adheres to a strict fitness regimen: every morning he wakes up at 4am for half an hour of jumping jacks, followed by a brisk walk with ankle weights. When he's not shopping for new speed-walking shoes at REI, you can find him roasting his own coffee beans at home. Nothing like a good cup of "joe" to get you revved up!

SKYLERR LINCOLN joined *Dad Magazine* as Deputy Editor in 2015 after the birth of his first daughter. Previously, Skylerr spent his summers embedded with the Capos in Sinaloa and his winters drinking Samogon with poachers in the Russian taiga. His work has appeared in *Sin*, *Razorblade*, and *Deprave*. He is the founding editor of Brooklyn's *2 Poems 4 U* Zine. Upon the birth of their daughter, the Lincolns immediately moved from Bushwick, Brooklyn, to Windsor, CT. Skylerr is excited to bring his trademark edge to the local Elks Lodge!

LETTER FROM THE
"DAD"ITOR

How's it hangin', Pops?

We're excited to bring you a very special issue this month, in honor of *Dad Magazine*'s centennial anniversary. Who would have thought that 100 years later, we'd still be going strong? I'm thrilled to be a part of this venerable institution's legacy, and to be able to watch it grow through the launch of our sister publications: Moms Monthly and Weird Uncle Living. (If you haven't subscribed, you don't know what you're missing!)

When I signed on as the Editor in Chief of *Dad Magazine*, I had one mission: to ensure dads everywhere had a voice. With every issue I feel that voice is getting stronger, and that Paternal Americans have a place to engage with and discuss the topics that matter to them. Whether it's the outrageous speed of your neighbors' driving, ordering appetizers for the group when you go out to dinner, or setting up your fantasy football league the old-fashioned way (i.e., with giant whiteboards in your basement), we're proud to be your magazine. I'm also so pleased to include the voices of all types of dads out there through a growing and diverse set of contributors and readers. I'd like to give a "shout-out" to the growing numbers of Dads Married to Dads (DMDs) in our readership. Don't forget to order a second subscription!

There have been some changes at *Dad Magazine* recently. After 20 years as Non-Contact Sports Editor, Ed Winston announced his retirement. We'll be sad to see him go, but he'll be pursuing his true passion: fly fishing. If you're around Montana's Gallatin River, look him up! With that said, we'd like to warmly welcome Ed's replacement, Larry Sheehan! Larry hails from Fond du Lac, Wisconsin, where he spends his time ice fishing, bowling, and taking his kayak out on Lake Winnebago. Larry comes to us after years of great work at *Dads Illustrated*, and we know his expertise and enthusiasm will be great assets to our editorial team.

As always, by dads, for dads.

Sincerely,

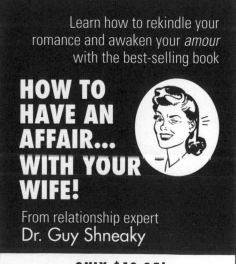
LETTERS
FROM OUR READERS

Dads from around the country Sound Off!

Loved your last issue, especially the "15 Great New Websites For Dads" article. This "Yelp" thing is pretty useful!

— *Dave, Pine Bluff, AR*

What was with "Dad Rock For Dads Who Rock"? Dads can listen to cool music, too! For instance, I just discovered this band, Smashing Pumpkins, last week. Not all of us are out of touch.

— *Carl, Sacramento, CA*

I loved last month's feature on this year's alarm clocks! Talk about news I can use!!!! ;-) I know I'll never miss the best part of any day.

— *Jeff, New Milford, CT*

Thank you so much for May's article about the health perks of not paying attention! ["9 Health Benefits of Tuning out Your Kids" - Ed.] I continued to tune my kids out that month like normal, but have felt more energized and almost made it through the entire evening's programming slate without falling asleep in my armchair! Thanks, *DadMag*!

— *Nick, Mt. Desert Island, ME*

I'm sorry, but I have to take issue with the January *DadMag* Quiz ["What's Your Beer Style?" - Ed.] I took the quiz and the results were clearly in favor of "IPA" when I've favored pilsners my whole life. Please know that those of us who enjoy a refreshing brew are not a monolith, and some of us prefer a more subtle flavor in our beers.

— *Steve, Hannibal, MO*

While I'm glad *Dad Mag* finally covered the epidemic of short-statured leading men in Hollywood ("Why So Many Actors Today Are Just Pretending to Be That Tall"), I do need to point out that this is NOT a new phenomenon. Everyone knows Bogie had to stand on a box to film *Casablanca!!* Please do your research next time.

— *Roger, Winter Harbor, ME*

CORRECTIONS:
POBODY'S NERFECT!

• In "We'll Make Up The Time on the Highway: Important Roadside Destinations!" we listed the world's largest community-rolled ball of twine as the ball in Alexandria, Indiana. That distinction actually belongs to the town of Cawker City, Kansas. Alexandria is, of course, throne to the world's largest ball of paint.

• Our "Great Marinades to Brag About" piece mistakenly called for rosemary in our "Fancy French" marinade. We meant tarragon! Quel domage, right?

• We reported that readers voted Steely Dan "Artist of the Year 2015" with 62% of the vote. Upon further review, it was actually 76%. Bill Withers was a close second with 24%.

DAD OF THE MONTH

DAD STATS

Name: David Huang

Age: 39

Location: Albuquerque, NM

Height: 5'8"

Weight: 170

Hat Size: 8

Favorite Sports Team: New Mexico State Aggies

Favorite Tool: Oscillating dremel

Favorite Battery Size: C

Favorite Shoe Insert Style: Half-arch all the way!

Favorite Car Accessory: Reflective window shade

Hey, there!
Well, howdy!

What's your story?
Well, I live with my wife, daughter, and son right here in Albuquerque. It's almost hatch chile season! What a time to be alive.

What's your favorite part about being a dad?
Oh, definitely making pancakes for the kiddo. Hey, you ever put chiles in your syrup? Hoo-eee, that'll wake you up!

So you like cooking for your kids?
Absolutely. It's a great way to bond, plus they're definitely the only kids in their school showing up with lamb curry instead of boring ol' ham sandwiches. I bet they're the coolest kids there!

What's one thing you've learned from being a dad?
You gotta be a leader. Some days your kids just won't want to watch *Starship Troopers* again, but you have to remind yourself they'll be grateful for the memories later.

Tell us a joke!
You hear the Energizer bunny got arrested? He was charged with battery!

DAD JOKES

This month:

SON: Dad, I'm starving. Can you make me a sandwich?
DAD (clapping his hands): Abbracadabra! You're a sandwich!

Q: How much does a hipster weigh?
A: An instagram!

KEEPING UP WITH THE KIDS

This month:
UPDATE YOUR LINGO!

INSTEAD OF: "Groovy"   **SAY:** "LOL!"
FOR EXAMPLE: "That internet webpage you sent me is totally LOL! Good work."

INSTEAD OF: "Catch you on the flip-side!"
SAY: "Hasta la vista, baby!"
FOR EXAMPLE: "I'm leaving the restaurant now. Hasta la vista, baby!"

INSTEAD OF: "Boogie"   **SAY:** "Krumping"
FOR EXAMPLE: "You hear about that new Krump, the macarena?"

INSTEAD OF: Calling someone a "cat"
SAY: "bro"
FOR EXAMPLE: "That is one groovy bro"

DID YOU KNOW?

Why is a PHILLIPS SCREWDRIVER called a phillips screwdriver?

The answer: it's named after someone named Phillips! **HENRY F. PHILLIPS**, of Portland, OR, invented the x-shaped socket head screw. After a trial run on the 1936 Cadillac, it became very popular in the auto industry, and quickly became the most popular screw in the world.

The birth of WD-40

In 1953, the Rocket Chemical Company in San Diego set out to create degreasers and rust solvents for the aerospace industry. After 40 attempts to perfect a water displacement formula, WD-40 (Water Displacement, 40th formula) was born. The same formula is still used today.

Who ate MISTER DONUT?

Founded in 1955, the popular donut chain was digested by Dunkin' Donuts in 1990, with the last remaining North American Mister Donut in Godfrey, IL. Throughout the rest of the world, however, it remains one of the largest donut franchises.

A teaspoon of matter from a neutron star weighs more than

357 TRILLION BASEBALLS

Believe it or not, the standard Rubik's Cube has

43,252,003,274,489,856,000

different possible configurations, and every single one can be solved in 20 moves or fewer (if you are some sort of a genius, that is).

The SHORTEST WAR on record:

Anglo-Zanzibar war of 1896, which only lasted 38 minutes.

VITAL STATS

According to a recent scientific survey:
DAD MOWS THE LAWN 25% of the time
DAD MAKES THE KIDS MOW THE LAWN 75% of the time

An official study has found that:
DAD IS ALWAYS RIGHT 75% of the time
DAD'S WRONG (but won't admit it) **20%** of the time
THE KIDS ARE RIGHT 5% of the time

DUCT TAPE was originally called

DUCT TAPE was originally called **DUCK TAPE** and was army green, not silver. It was named "duck tape" because it was waterproof, like a duck, and made with cotton duck fabric.

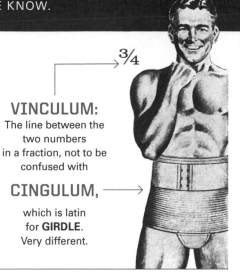

$3/4$

VINCULUM:
The line between the two numbers in a fraction, not to be confused with

CINGULUM,
which is latin for **GIRDLE**. Very different.

BOWLING JARGON

TURKEY: three strikes in a row

HAM BONE: four strikes in a row

WILD TURKEY: six strikes in a row

GOLDEN TURKEY: nine strikes in a row

DINOSAUR: perfect twelve strikes in a row

The lint that collects in the bottom of your pockets has a name:

GNURR

The lint in your belly-button does not.

Has a male ever given birth? The answer is YES!

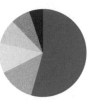

In the undersea world of the seahorse, the male is the one that gets pregnant and gives birth the babies.

Napoleon was once **attacked by rabbits.** We're not kidding.

DAD TO THE RESCUE

In 1950, Harry Truman came to his daughter's defense after the *Washington Post* gave her singing a bad review, replying to the critic:

"Some day I hope to meet you. When that happens you'll need a new nose, a lot of beefsteak for black eyes, and perhaps a supporter below!"

When it comes to home repairs, Dad:

KNOWS HOW & DOES IT HIMSELF 50%
DOESN'T KNOW HOW & CALLS REPAIRMAN 5%
DOESN'T KNOW but tries, disastrously 45%

READERS POLL

This month:
WHO DO YOU LOOK TO FOR DAD-SPIRATION?

54% **MY DAD**
16% **I JUST WING IT**
12% **JOE NAMATH**
8% **JOHN WAYNE'S DAD**
6% **MIKE BRADY**
4% **ARCHIE BUNKER**

KEEP A LIST

This month:
THINGS THAT DO NOT GROW ON TREES

We all know money doesn't grow on trees. Well, all of us except for my damn kids, who think of me as some sort of walking, talking, sweater-wearing ATM. You know what else doesn't grow on trees? Everything listed here:

- Fancy jeans
- Expensive sneakers
- Brand-name soda
- Pizza with all the toppings (*Isn't plain good enough?*)
- The most expensive thing on the menu
- Separate shampoo and conditioner (*What's wrong with all-in-one?*)
- Electricity
- Heat
- Air conditioning
- Prom dresses
- One Direction tickets
- College tuition
- JSTOR accounts
- Video games
- Baseball gloves
- Baseball cards
- Printer ink
- Fancy phones (*What's wrong with my old pager?*)
- Fancy phone accessories (*like the phone isn't fancy enough?*)
- Netflix accounts
- A new car

ASK A DAD

Each month, we choose a new dad to answer your most pressing questions. This month's dad is Norm, a repairman from Lamar, Colorado.

Dear Dad,

I want to make sure my kids get a good education, both inside and outside of school. What topics would you suggest I teach them that standard public education doesn't normally cover?

Best,
Bob

Dear Bob,
Schools are great for teaching things like dodgeball and that one Hemingway book that wasn't so bad, but at home is where kids develop the practical knowledge of everyday life, so the sky is really the limit! Given that I'm an Eagle Scout, I think "be prepared" is a great mission statement for your home education. Teach them the value of carrying an extra $20 in their wallet for emergencies, and leaving chocolate bars around the house in case of a sudden case of low blood sugar.

Dear Dad,

My wife and I are expecting our first child! I'm really excited to be a dad, and want to make sure I do a good job, but sometimes I get worried, because it seems like there's just so much to know. What tips do you have for young, new dads?

Best,
Kevin

Dear Kevin,
Congratulations to you and your wife! Firstly, don't worry, every dad has experienced what you're going through. In some ways it never stops! Every time I think I'm doing a good job as a dad, I remember something I forgot to do, like making them listen to the Smothers Brothers. It's all a learning experience, and your parenting style will continue to change as your child grows. Sometimes you'll be the embarrassing mall dad, and other times you'll be the dad who refuses to pull over during a road trip because you stopped three times already. All of these facets of your dadhood need to be balanced and utilized appropriately. Try to think of it like a big tacklebox: don't use a spoon lure when you need a spinner! Remember, there is no one single Dad for All Seasons.

Dear Dad,

As I get older, I'm finding that time is slipping by imperceptibly faster and faster. I used to be able to savor each morning and evening with my family, but with my advancing age and the speed of today's world, I feel like I'm hitting the bed to go to sleep just as soon as I'm finally awake!

Anyways, what size wrench should I use for a 7/16 bolt?

Best,
Ron

Dear Ron,
⅝".

....

Dear Dad,

Something is going on with my 14-year-old daughter. She used to love it when I'd make up silly lyrics to popular songs and sing them at her sleepovers, but lately she seems annoyed by it. She also spends most of her time in her room on family chess night. What gives?

Best,
Frank

Dear Frank,
Ahhh, jeez. Uhh, maybe she's on her period? My, would you look at the time.

Have a question for next month's dad? Send your query to:
dads_question_dadofthemonth_ihaveaquestion@excite.com with the subject line "I have a question!"

Want to BE next month's dad? Send a writing sample and headshot to:
dads_question_answer_iwant2bethedadofthemonth@hotmail.com with the subject line "I've got the answers!"

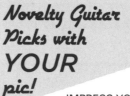

FAUX "PA"S

Dads tell us their most embarrassing stories!

Take the Edge Off

A few weekends ago I headed down to the hardware store–I was picking up supplies to build a better debris shield for my string trimmer (you know how they're never protective enough!). Anyway, I get home and find that I accidentally took the measurements from my edge trimmer, not string trimmer! Boy was my face red!

— Stan, Bowling Green, KY

International Man of Misery

My wife and I love hosting parties, especially since it gives us an opportunity to show off our cooking skills with some appetizing appetizers. At our last party, we decided to really blow out all the stops and cook spanakopita, a regional Greek delicacy made with spinach, feta and phyllo dough. It looked beautiful, and we got so many compliments, but I guess the feta must have been out of date because all of our guests wound up getting food poisoning that night! What a blooper!

— Chris, Brookline, MA

Shortcut Slip Up

Like many dads, I appreciate a good bargain, which is why I resolved to always go to the Stop & Shop two towns over instead of our grocery store— their milk is regularly fifteen cents cheaper than in my own. However, one afternoon I was short on time, and I had to pick up groceries from the local store. I bet I paid an extra $6 total. I still haven't told my wife!

— Jeff, Glen Ridge, NJ

Radio Redirection

My morning commute can be somewhat of a hassle, so I like to have a few creature comforts with me: my back pillow, my thermos of coffee, and of course talk radio. Last week I was particularly fascinated by a segment on the nature of free market capitalism, and I admit, between the comfort of my seat and the riveting conversation, I got distracted and wound up off-course by two hours! Oops!

— Carl, Ogden, UT

Have an embarrassing story? Send yours to: embarrassing_story_dads45_dadmagthemagazine@earthlink.net **and put the entire story in the subject line.**

WHAT'S YOUR FAVORITE TALK RADIO SHOW?

You wrote in and here are your results!

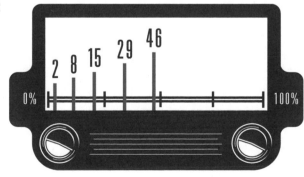

46%	**Chuck and The Toaster on WSPORTS RADIO**
29%	**The Beau Limrose Show, KGOP**
15%	**Whisperin' about the Arts, American Public Radio**
8%	**Traffic on the 8's**
2%	**Get Your Goat with "Farmer John" Hubbns (HAM Radio Only)**

LOOK WHAT I FOUND

Who are you? Frank Stetson, Barrington, NH. Proud father of three dogs and two kids.

What did you find? A mounted Jackalope head. What a trophy!

How did you find it? I was going through my garage trying to find my 9 Piece Industrial-Grade combination ratchet wrench set and I stumbled across it at the bottom of an old shelving unit.

How are you gonna use it? Well, first of all, the little fella's pretty dusty from being in storage so long, and the wife's allergic to mold something fierce, so I'm probably gonna give him a good scrubdown with some industrial carpet shampoo. Maybe spiff up those little horns with some shoe polish, too. And then the possibilities are endless! Put a little American flag in his mouth for the Fourth of July, hang some fake spiderwebs on him for Halloween, dangle ornaments on the horns for Christmas... or a little Santa hat! That's the ticket. A man for all seasons, this guy!

Aren't you glad you didn't throw it away? Damn straight.

Who are you? Sam Ploszaj, Batavia, IL. Go Bears!

What did you find? An old fondue set! I haven't seen this thing in years. It was a wedding present from the Liebowitzes!

How did you find it? My wife and I were gonna get back into "juicing" after we saw something about it on *Doctor Oz*, so I went rooting around in the storage

area under the basement stairs for that contraption. I think it might have been claimed in a garage sale, but lo and behold! Our old fondue set.

How are you gonna use it? My doctor won't let me have cheese anymore—he says it's bad for the ol' ticker—but this thing can do so much more than just cheese! For instance, my youngest is big into Chemistry, so viola, a free science kit for Junior! She could melt down all sorts of wacky crap in there. Or maybe we fill it with flowers and soil and use it as a centerpiece at one of those dinner parties we keep talking about having.

Aren't you glad you didn't throw it away? You betcha!

Who are you? Edgar Soote, Wilkes-Barre, PA. It's pronounced "Wilkes BERRY." Make sure you put that in there.

What did you find? One of those squeezy stress guys! Bug-Out-Bob, I think he's called. Kinda looks like a little rubber clown, heh.

How did you find it? I was up in the attic, doing my annual bat corpse sweep when I got a wild hair up my ass to see what was in some of those dang boxes.

How are you gonna use it? Well, they're known stress relievers, but aside from that, all sorts of things! You could safely play catch inside the house. Or you could wrap it up and give to your granddaughter as a birthday present. Kids love this stuff! And squeezing is an important skill for toddlers.

Aren't you glad you didn't throw it away? Oh, yeah. For sure.

DADSHOTS

When Is That Tattoo Trend Going to Stop?

"Ehhh I don't get it, needles in your skin just to look like a hooligan."

—*Arnold, Bloomington, IN*

"What are you trying to say about that Elmer Fudd I got in college?"

—*Pete, Cedar Rapids, IA*

"I'd say 2058. Well, the late 2050's for absolute sure. Way I see it, extrapolating from current trends, at least sociopolitically and economically, all the kids now will be adults with tattoos. Every last stinkin' one of em. By that time, their kids will be growing up, and they'll see tattoos as something for oldsters. Best way to get my teenager to stop doing something is to say I like it! Buncha contrarians if you ask me. 2062, maybe."

—*Will, Lincoln, ME*

"A man has a right to do what he wants with his own body, which is why I haven't trimmed my moustache in two years."

—*Jim, Salem, OR*

"Stewed, Screwed and Tattooed, haha! What was the question?"

—*Harvey, Erie, PA*

Whatcha Doin' Down There?

"Tinkering!"

—*Mitch, Charleston, SC*

"I'm on a conference call, quit using the internet!"

—*Steve, Monroe, CT*

"Oh, you know…"

—*Craig, Anaheim, CA*

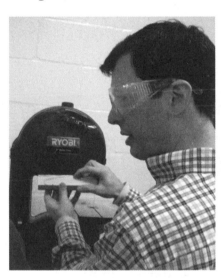

"Don't come down here! It's dangerous!"

—*Aditya, Terre Haute, IN*

"What don't I have going on down here? I've got a little gym setup with that treadmill—now watch out, the drop ceiling's low and you have to take out one of the tiles to run on it. I've got my spare desk and a separate phone line for getting work done, and I've got my workshop. I'll get that toaster oven fixed pretty soon!"

—*Nick, Huntsville, AL*

What Did You Want to Be When You Grew Up?

"The next Scott Hastings, Detroit Pistons power forward. Sure he wasn't considered 'good,' but he had so much hustle!"

—*Rafi, Ypsilanti, MI*

"Retired!"

—*Fritz, Conneautville, PA*

"I wanted to be…A LUMBERJACK! Haha, like from Monty Python, get it? C'mon, I got you those videos!"
—*Ken, Decatur, GA*

"Stern."

—*Al, Grand Junction, CO*

"Just what I am now—Senior Actuary for the Actuary Board of America!"

—*Chuck, Davenport, IL*

"I dreamed of being a manufacturing engineer as a child, but at some point I had to get practical, which is why I'm now a systems engineer. Yep, at some point we all gotta grow up."

—*Darell, Englewood, NJ*

SPORTS + FITNESS

SPORTS AIN'T WHAT THEY USED TO BE

We break down what's wrong

20

TACKLING YOUR TACKLE BOX

Get your hook, line, *and* sinker

22

GET SOME EXERCISE— YES, YOU!

What doesn't kill ya makes ya stronger

30

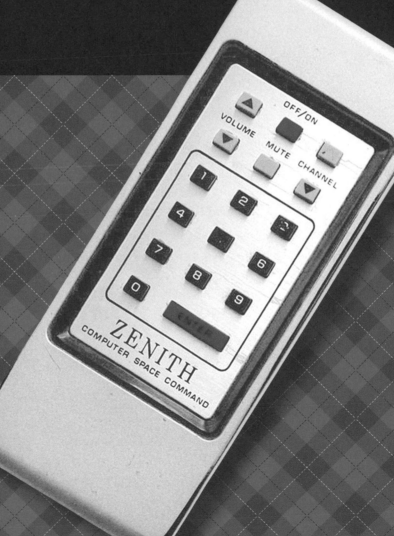

LATELY, EVERY SPORT HAS BEEN

Hi, sports fans. As you well know, sports, just like everything else, are not as good as they used to be when we were kids (whenever that was). Some people say this is subjective and due to your fearless author being bitter and old, but that's definitely not the case. Luckily for you, I've laid it all out by sport.

RUINED! FOOTBALL

Remember when pro football was just a bunch of hillbillies on amphetamines wrestling each other in the mud and snow while a little guy tried to run the ball up the middle for 2 yards? So do I! I remember when a forward pass was a rare thing to be marveled at, none of this exciting thirty to forty times a game nonsense we have now! It's a bunch of hooey —what, you want me to be overstimulated? The point of football is to sit in an armchair and eat chicken wings until I fall asleep, not to be *entertained*. Jeez!

And don't get me started on the players today! With their fancy-schmancy product placement deals and their mansions and nice cars. Back in my day, the players made so little money they had to drive trucks in the offseason to make ends meet, and maybe you opened a car dealership in rural Missouri after you retired at 34 from brain injuries. Now that's what I call smash-mouth football!

RUINED! BASEBALL

Remember when pro baseball was just a bunch of drunk, fatsos hitting ground balls that the pitcher coated in his own saliva to second base and trying to leg out a single? So do I! Now they've got all these fancy-pants "statistics" trying to tell me how good a player is! I've got one statistic for you, kid: I call it The Eye Test. What's he look like? Is he trying real hard? That's all I care about.

And don't get me started on the "defensive shift"! Back in my day, nobody used advanced field-tracking data to analyze and predict a player's natural tendencies to hit the ball in any direction in order to determine their defenders' positions on the field to prevent base hits! No! We just let the guy hit the ball in the same spot through the infield every time and we lost the games and were HAPPY ABOUT IT, Thank you very much.

RUINED!

And what are all these extra playoff games nowadays? More of the thing I like? *No Thanks.*

HOCKEY

Remember when pro hockey was a bunch of guys named Gord with mullets beating the snot out of each other while drunk Manitobans threw cans of Molson at at them? So do I! Now all the players are these Russian prima-donnas who are too busy looking at their own reflection in the glass to get back on defense! Disgraceful, if you ask me.

And don't get me started on fighting! Back in my day, you couldn't go a couple of minutes without someone getting their lights knocked out for looking at a guy the wrong way! I tried to watch a game last week and they just played hockey the whole time! What the heck, guys?

I remember when all the people that played sports were bad at them and worse uncomfortable clothing. But I guess those days are gone now. A sad time to be alive.

BASKETBALL

Remember when pro basketball was just a bunch of lanky weirdos bounce-passing the ball back and forth to each other and jogging slowly? I do! Now it's all these guys with *skills* shooting shots from far away and doing a "slam dunk," which I believe is a type of slang for placing the ball in the hoop. Preposterous.

And don't get me started on those shorts! If they're not going to stop mid-thigh, they're just weird pants, if you ask me.

THE GREAT HANDS HALL OF FAME

Most professional athletes have hands. But only some out there have had the true gift of Great Hands. Today, we honor those men.

JERRY RICE: That guy could catch a marble in a rainstorm.

STEVE LARGENT: This guy ran as fast as my grandmother but he must've had glue on his hands!

LYNN SWANN: You see that one catch? Now THAT is what I call a catch! Good hands? No. Great.

MICHAEL IRVIN: Incredible hands. Some of the best we've ever seen. Sure, he stabbed his own teammate with a pair of scissors, but think about the grip strength you'd need for that!

TACKLE BOX GUIDE

by **LARRY SHEEHAN**

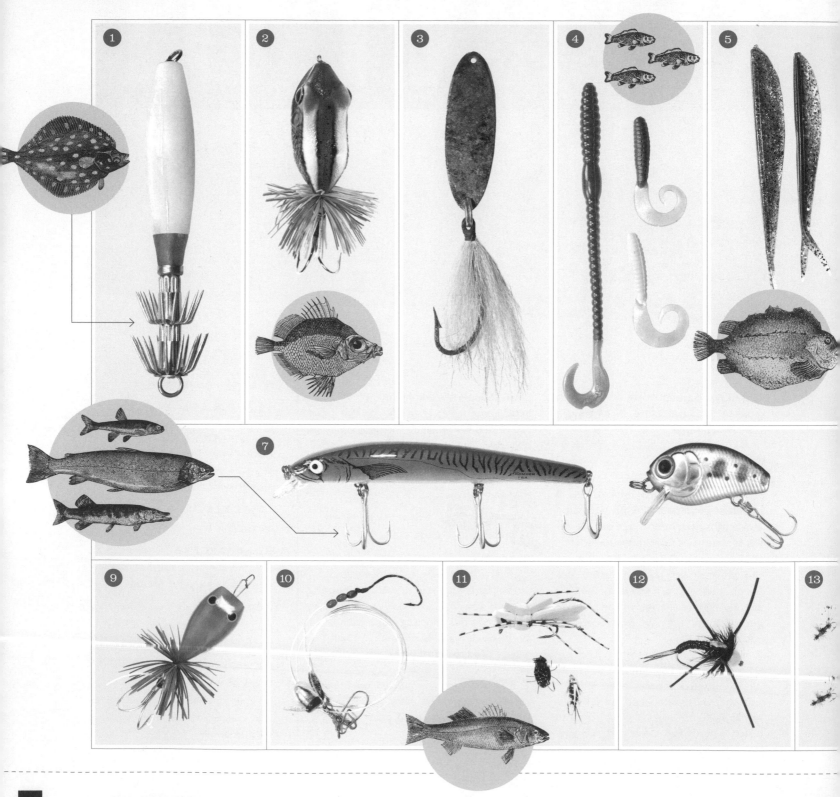

Hello, anglers! A lot of dads love to fish, but most don't realize they're working with a severe handicap. That's right—tacklebox selection and organization. A well-stocked tacklebox can handle any situation your favorite river, lake, or ocean can throw at you. And having everything in the right place can save you time. Time you could be fishing, which we all know takes hour upon grueling hour of leisurely drinking and chatting. Time is fishes, as they say!

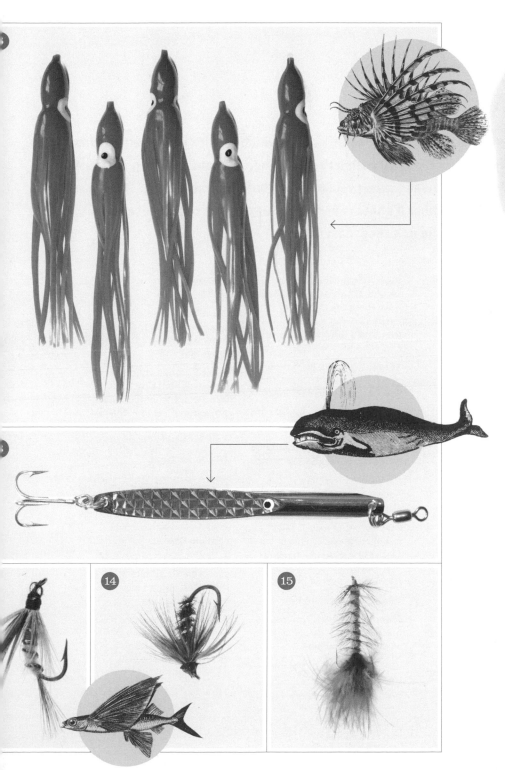

1. **CRANKBAITS**

2. **TWEAKBAIT**

3. **JERKBAITS:** For your more stubborn fish—you know what we're talking about!

4. **SYNTHETI-WORM:** Coulda fooled us! This thing looks just like a worm. Check out that worm-like shape! Wow.

5. **TWERKBAIT**

6. **WIGGLEWRIGGLES:** Though the two are indistinguishable to human eyes, this jig's patented alternating wiggling and wriggling motions will trick just about any fish!

7. **SNAGTHRUSTS**

8. **YANKBAIT**

9. **QUAKE-N-FISH**

10. **JIGGARIGS:** The Jig that won't give up™

11. **FIZZETAIL GRUB**

12. **WOBBLIN' JOE**

13. **HURDY-GURDY-MAN**

14. **BANGARANG**

15. **FLOBBLE-FLEEG**

YOUR BEST

HUNTING WEEKEND ITINERARY

by **LARRY SHEEHAN**   *Illustration by* **CSA ARCHIVE**

If there's two things I love, it's hunting and crafting intricate itineraries from which my kids are not allowed to stray, not even for a second, because we have a schedule to stick to gosh dangit. Because hunting isn't just for filling up the three freezers in the garage with sweet, sweet venison; it's a bonding experience. These are the memories the kids will keep for a lifetime, whether it's how to perfectly skin a rabbit to remembering that Rusty is the one that gives you a nice discount at the bait shop, not Frank.

FRIDAY

4am: Rouse the family from their slumber and head to the car. You'll eat on the road. Also, you packed the night before (see the How To on page 96 for good car packing tips).

5am: Time for breakfast. From now on, everyone is on a steady ration of jerky, trail mix, and water while not on the campsite. (On the campsite, it's strictly hot dogs.)

5:30am: By now the troops might be getting a little restless, so pull over for some leg exercises. Don't want anyone getting that deep vein thrombosis!

6am: Continue driving to the campsite.

6:15am: Get lost.

6:20am: Back on track!

6:30am: Get lost again. It builds character!

9am: Finally back on track.

10am: Arrive at the campsite! Take an hour to find the perfect place to pitch a tent. You're going to want to measure the distance to the nearest water source, determine ground density, and contact the park rangers about the specific coordinates for bear attacks in the past ten years. Safety first!

Noon: By now you should have figured out a campsite and gotten everyone settled. But don't "chill out" for too long! You'll get hunting bright and early, but the rest of the day is for intricate gun- and crossbow-safety drills and knot-tying contests.

2pm: Around now your kids may be getting hungry, but withhold food until they can produce a convincing call of a mating female mallard.

5pm: Time to start thinking of dinner, which dovetails with that classic family activity— building a fire together! Don't cheat with lighter fluid, though; you know there's nothing like a flame made from sticks, string, and some dry leaves. The three hours it takes will absolutely be worth it.

8pm: Hot dog time!

9pm: To get everyone ready for bed, tell some scary stories. How about the one about the hunter who didn't take his gun-safety drills seriously and shot himself in the leg?

10pm: Lights out for everyone else, but you vow to stay up until 3am to guard against bears.

10:30pm: Fall asleep while on watch.

SATURDAY

5:30am: Rouse the troops! They'll be grateful you let them sleep in.

6:30am: After a quick breakfast of hot dogs, it's time to hunt! Stake out a good hiding spot and wait for the game, whether it's whitetail deer or pheasant.

10am: Keep waiting!

Noon: Remember, you're teaching your kids patience as much as anything.

2pm: Relinquish some trail mix if they're getting cranky.

3:45pm: Why not play a game while you wait? Start counting the leaves on the trees. First one to 100 wins!

5:30pm: Better luck next time, right?

6pm: You may not have caught anything today, but you know what makes that better? Hot dogs!

8pm: Surprise your kids with a special treat: s'mores! Be sure not to let them have a marshmallow until they've demonstrated their even-browning technique.

10pm: Bedtime.

SUNDAY

5am: Up, up, up! Gotta hit the road if you want to make it home in time for the game!

6am: Finish cleaning up the campsite. Be sure to leave no trace, or if you do leave a trace, bury it really deep.

6:30am: While you're driving, this is a good opportunity to explain to your kids that you didn't even want to kill anything anyway.

1pm: Arrive home, just in time for the game. Make your kids unload the car.

HOW GOOD IS THE SUN?

Illustration by **HEADCASE DESIGN**

GET OUT THERE AND SOAK UP THE SUN!

by **BARRY BUCKET**

Ahhh, the great outdoors. There's nothing better than getting out of your musty old house to play catch with your kids, kayak at a nearby pond, or just relax on the beach. Even in the winter months, you can go for a refreshing ice skate on a clear day. You know why these activities invigorate the soul? The sun! That's right, there's nothing that can't be made better by catching some rays.

Did you know that President Teddy Roosevelt was a sickly child? It's true! He suffered all sorts of weaknesses and ailments. Luckily his father realized the power of sunlight, taking young Teddy hiking and camping. Soon this asthmatic child was boxing foreigners and wrestling bears!

Our magnificent sun provides sustenance for our plants, and Vitamin D for our bones. It keeps our planet temperate and gives us beautiful sunsets. It even powers those solar walkway lamps I ordered from SkyMall. So why would I want to shield myself from it with sunscreen, hats, or sunglasses? If Ra wanted us to use sunscreen, he would have invented it himself.

I hear a lot of hooey about the damage the sun can do. Sure, we've all had a dozen or so age spots removed because of "pre-cancerous cells," but what good is having a sun if you spend all your time avoiding its warm embrace? Without the sun, we'd all be dead, so let's get out there and appreciate it!

Fact!

Zinc oxide is a natural inhibitor of mold and fungi! But don't worry, wearing it still makes you a fun guy.

Zinc Oxide

GET IN HERE AND HIDE FROM THE SUN!

by **HUGO RANDALL**

Joseph Stalin had a "Great Plan for the Transformation of Nature" in 1940s Russia, which was built on the idea that the natural world is a valuable thing—if you can control it. Now I'm no Communist, but the man had a point, especially when it comes to sunlight! Yes our sun gives us warmth and light, but let us never forget that it's hellbent on killing us all.

I first discovered the dangers of the sun on a skiing trip, when I came off the slopes with the worst sunburn I'd ever had. It wasn't even warm out! The sun was a sneak, and the cultural assumption that we should only block ourselves from its rays on sunny beach days was one way it had tricked me.

Between the hole in the Ozone layer and that extra hour of cursed sunlight Daylight Savings gives us, I never leave the house without at least a wide-brimmed hat, an SPF undershirt, polarized sunglasses and a hefty swipe of zinc oxide down my nose, and I certainly don't let my family leave the house unprotected either.

A lot of people will try to tell you that sunlight is good for you, but to me the risks far outweigh the good. So get in here and let's play some Parcheesi next to my industrial-strength sun lamp. I promise you won't be able to tell the difference!

Online Poll:

WHAT DO YOU DO ABOUT THE SUN?

23% Slather on the sunblock

21% Never go outside

28% I've always been fine without protection! Grow up.

25% Whatever happened to going tanning?

3% One time, I burned the bald spot on my head. Ouch!

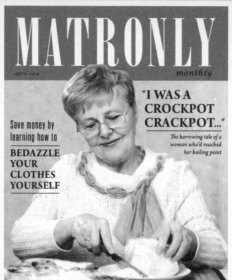

INTRODUCING THE NEWEST (yet oldest)

MEMBER OF OUR FAMILY:

GREAT GRANDAD

OCTOBER 2016   MAGAZINE

PREMIERE ISSUE!

WANT TO WIN AT BINGO: have we got some tips for you!

5 OF THE HOTTEST MOBILITY SCOOTERS
ON THE MARKET

10 GREAT WAYS
you & your family can tell if your new fiancée is

IN IT JUST FOR THE MONEY!

COUNTRY-STYLE LEMONADE IS MAKING A COMEBACK!

 Write now for a **FREE TRIAL ISSUE** at no cost to you!

HEALTH HACKS

TRICK YOUR BODY INTO BEING HEALTHY

by **GERALD WEN**

Photos by **MICHAEL REALI**

We all know 30 minutes of cardio a day helps keep our hearts strong and our bodies limber—not to mention giving us a better chance of beating the neighbor's son on the morning run. He got back from college last month and just thinks he's so great, but you'll show him! The problem is, half an hour is a lot of time, and sometimes it gets hard to manage. But what if you could maximize your exercise potential by incorporating it into your everyday tasks?

"The body responds more powerfully to multitasking than it does to any one activity," according to Dr. Frederick Mumenschanz, Professor of Paternal Health at the University of Heidelberg and inventor of the elliptical-powered fax machine. "By tricking your body into exercising while doing otherwise mundane tasks, you force your body to build muscle and burn calories before it even realizes it's doing work."

Shout for your kids to come downstairs and clean up their crap, and then jog in place until they get there.

COME CLEAN UP YOUR CRAP!

continue for approx. 20 minutes

repeat until you get yelled at

Enjoying a friendly game at the bowling alley? Try shot-putting the ball as far as you can when it isn't your turn! (Not responsible for broken lanes or heads.)

don't forget to breathe!

Add resistance by tying weights to your ankles for extra abdominal exercise as you get ready to relax.

until you can't breathe

Use that heavy toolbox to get in as many "reps" of exercise as you can stand.

x 50 reps

x 25 reps

When you're on your hands and knees looking for that DARN remote, why not do a few pushups?

perfect posture

hold, change channel x 10

perfect posture for napping

Screaming about the game? Grab a free weight while you're waving your arms around.

Needlessly re-arrange the boxes in the attic 3 or 4 times a week—the really heavy ones.

THE HEART OF THE MATTER

As we Dads get older, heart health is an ongoing concern. Research has shown that up to 100% of people without working hearts risk death. We've pinpointed some of the biggest risk factors that Dads today face and laid them out below. Remember: A healthy Dad is an *effective* Dad!

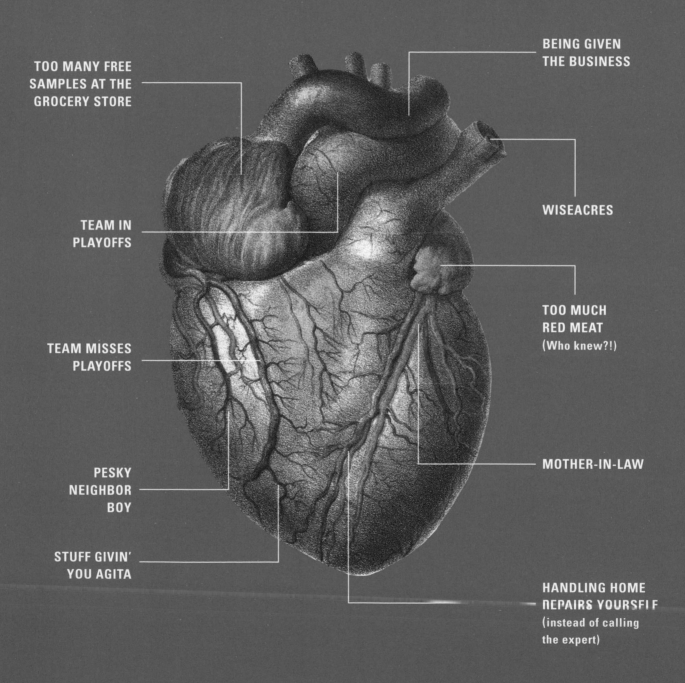

TOO MANY FREE SAMPLES AT THE GROCERY STORE

BEING GIVEN THE BUSINESS

TEAM IN PLAYOFFS

WISEACRES

TEAM MISSES PLAYOFFS

TOO MUCH RED MEAT (Who knew?!)

PESKY NEIGHBOR BOY

MOTHER-IN-LAW

STUFF GIVIN' YOU AGITA

HANDLING HOME REPAIRS YOURSELF (instead of calling the expert)

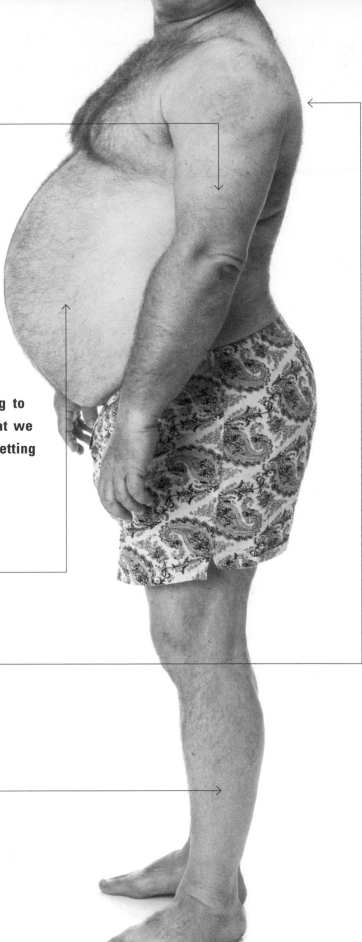

**GETTING THINGS
DOWN FROM THE ATTIC
ALL THE TIME**
(even though you specifically
asked everyone to just make a
big list to minimize trips)

FATHER FIGURE

by **DADMAG STAFF**

Our kids tell us that having a dad-like body is something to aspire to nowadays. Glad the world has caught up to what we dads have known all along! Here are some easy tricks to getting the DadBod of your dreams.

EATING A WHOLE PIZZA
(but only *after* you've
worked out)

RAISING CHILDREN
(Parenthood takes its toll on
your once-indomitable spirit
and provides a slightly
hunched posture.)

**THESE ARE JUST FINE
THE WAY THEY ARE,
THANK YOU**

DE LUXE TOASTER OVEN by TOASTMEISTER

Great for toast...

...but not just for toast!

If you have a toaster oven in your kitchen, you've likely been ignoring a world of possibilities. Toaster ovens are for more than just browning your bread; They're multi-taskers of the first degree. Just look at all these things your toaster oven can do:

Dry wet shoes/socks*   **Impromptu space heater***   **Boil water (albeit slowly)***

and more!

Head to wherever fine oven alternatives are sold today to find out all the ways you can use your toaster oven. And if you don't already have one, send away to TOASTMEISTER for our free catalog!

FOOD + DRINK

BREW-HA-HA!

Our guide to brewing your own beer.

37

EATING-OUT TIPS!

Why you should save your best jokes for the waitstaff.

43

MY FIRST GRILL

One man remembers the grill that set his heart aflame.

46

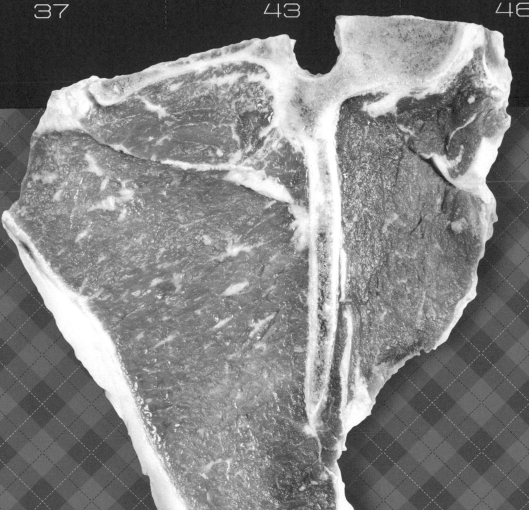

HOW TO

MAKE BEER IN YOUR BASEMENT

—THE DAD WAY!

by **MARTY WURLITZER**   Photo by **MICHAEL REALI**

A lot of my buddies have been asking me how I make my patented "Marty's Double-Hopped Boiler Room Saison," given that not four years ago I was about as green to beer brewing as a kitten to a karate chop. Yes sir, I had just about zero beverage production experience, unless you count the summers I ran a lemonade stand with my brother. Best darn lemonade in town, I say! That's because we made it the old-fashioned way...

"A quart of ale is a dish for a king."

—*William Shakespeare*

... with real lemons! None of this powdered lemon flavored product nonsense. I tell you, people used to be mighty wary of that stuff when I was younger, but then the government started getting involved with the food labels and now everyone and their grandmother thinks it's honest-to-god lemonade. Can you believe it?

Right, back to making beer! The first thing you want to do is figure out what type of beer you want to make. Any good beer is made of four basic ingredients—water, yeast, malt, and hops—but it's the combinations that make them different. You got your hoppy IPAs and your smooth wheat beers and your meaty stouts, and nowadays some people even put fruits in there. But the main thing to remember is that you don't need one of those fancy kits they advertise in the catalogs! Now, it takes a little elbow grease to find all the ingredients, but you do enough snoopin' around and you're bound to find more than enough to make a few good batches.

Right this way for instructions
on making your own brewski
from the Dad Mag Test Kitchen

YOU'LL NEED:

SOAP: You don't want any gunk muckin' up the works!

POT: For boiling wort! You gotta boil the wort.

SOMETHING TO FERMENT THE BEER IN: It's gotta have a firm seal! Otherwise, your beer might oxidize. I always thought it was funny that "oxidization" was a bad thing. Isn't oxygen good? I tell you, I just don't understand science.

SPOON: Just any spoon. Heck, use a fork.

AUTO SIPHON: When I first got into this, the siphons were all MANUAL. But you know, I'm getting older and the kids

want to do something else that's "easier," let 'em do it.

HYDROMETER: This is just a fancy word for a specific gravity measur-er! I don't see why this needs to get so pretentious.

BOTTLES: For bottling!

BOTTLE CAPPERS: Most guys will tell you that you need this to get the caps securely on the beer bottles but THOSE guys haven't had an ounce of hardship in their entire lives! The good lord gave you two hands, lazybones!

BOTTLE CAPS: Okay, you probably need these.

MAKING YOUR BREW

Okay, now to make the beer. What you want to do is wash everything out with that soap, and then boil your malt and your hops and whatever else you want to throw in there with about five gallons of water. Other people will tell you a lot more steps about "flavor" and "safety" and "explosions" and whatnot, but I'll tell you something: when you're in the battlefield, you're not worried about instructions, you're worried about survival! You got a gut feeling! So once you boil all that stuff together, you're going to want to put it in whatever you got to ferment it in, seal it off with the gravity doo-dad, and just let it sit. Easy-peasy!

Once the gravity thing stops bubbling up and calms down (just over a week, usually), you should be good to go. All that's left to do is add some sugar, attach your siphon, and start filling and capping those bottles! This should be good for a few dozen bottles, at least a dozen of which will explode in your pantry, so make sure to have a lot of towels handy!

NAMING YOUR BREW

Here it is: the piece de resistance, your beer's name! This is what people will remember you for, when the sun's flame is extinguished and humankind is but a distant memory of a memory. There are a couple naming conventions you could go with:

ALLITERATION: The thinking man's word for using the same letter at the front of a word twice! Makes you sound sophisticated, the sort of man that owns a thesaurus.

Examples: **Dan's Detroit Dunkel, Lambert's Lambic**

PUNS: Always good for a laugh! Puns never go out of style.

Examples: **The Beer from IPAnema; Stout, Stout, Let It All Out; Mario Puzo's The GodLager**

RHYMING: Another option for the wordsmiths out there. Conveys a playfulness that a mere alliteration won't.

Examples: **Whale Ale, What-a-Nice'n-Hefeweizen, This Year's Weissbier**

JUST PUT YOUR NAME IN FRONT OF THE WORD BEER: Not everyone out there is Shakespeare, for crying out loud! Also ensures that nobody forgets the master craftsman behind their delicious beverage.

Examples: **Rudy's Beer, Hal's Beer**

 Xerox or scan this handy-dandy template to make your own labels and impress the guys at poker!

LOOK AT THIS

NEW PIZZA STONE!

by **JOHN FRANGELICO**

SURE, you got your food processors, your woks, and your coffee grinders, but I don't think you can call yourself a "foodie" unless you've gotten yourself a real ceramic pizza stone. Check out the one I got recently. Finally, my kitchen is complete. Look out, Papa John's! Here comes a REAL papa. Named John! Too funny.

I first realized the necessity for a pizza stone when my son got engaged, and he and his wife-to-be began receiving gifts. Lo and behold, two different relatives sent them fancy pizza stones, and I thought, "Hey, why don't I have one of those?" What else could combine the dough starter I keep in the basement and those skills I learned at cheesemongering camp (the best $900 money can buy! A magical weekend in Palo Alto). I immediately emailed my son and, after some back-and-forth, finally convinced him to send me his extra stone. Flat-rate shipping, my friends! Can't recommend it enough.

You wouldn't believe the quality of pizza you can get out of this. Unlike a metal baking sheet, the ceramic pulls excess moisture out of the dough, giving you that perfect crust. The mozzarella will stay stringy and light on your classic pizza margherita, and you'll get even bubbling and browning all around. Just like Grandma made! Mmm, yes, I can see it now, serving pizza topped with prosciutto and gorgonzola on Poker Night, or perhaps with sweet potato sauce and turkey for a Thanksgiving surprise. Oh, or brie and tarragon for Bastille Day! Really, the sky's the limit with what you can do. Unless of course you want my youngest, John Jr., to eat it! Man, that kid is picky.

I haven't actually used it yet but I'll let you know how it goes. *Abbondanza!*

DADS FAVORITE PIZZA FLAVORS

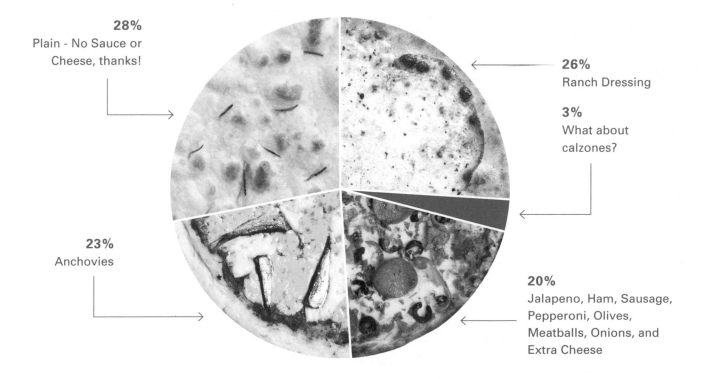

28%
Plain - No Sauce or Cheese, thanks!

26%
Ranch Dressing

3%
What about calzones?

23%
Anchovies

20%
Jalapeno, Ham, Sausage, Pepperoni, Olives, Meatballs, Onions, and Extra Cheese

DADMAG TREND WATCH

by **HARRY FROELICH**

FOOD: HERE'S A LOOK AT WHAT NONSENSE PEOPLE INSIST ON EATING THESE DAYS

Raise your hand if you were raised on a steady diet of beef stew and baked potatoes! There's not much more a dad needs to be happy, save for the occasional beer or experimental pickle. But nowadays there are a slew of culinary trends you and your family need to navigate. To make it easier, we've made this handy guide on the latest in food fads.

VEGETARIANISM

This is the practice of not eating meat (we know, wild!). Don't worry, it turns out there are plenty of things to eat on this diet. Pie, mashed potatoes, and coffee are all things considered vegetarian, and you can even replace the meat in your diet with vegetables. Instead of that hot dog, fill a bun with potato chips and ketchup—your family won't know the difference!

LOCAL FOOD

Nowadays, all the restaurants are saying that the food is "local" and "organic" and "sustainable" and "aioli" or something. Is the grocery store not local anymore? I mean, there's that weird store on the other side of town with the big chalkboard signs everywhere and the big barrels of grain or whatever. I bet all the chefs are shopping there.

WRAPS

If you haven't heard, too many carbs can be bad for you, so instead of traditional bread, some people like to eat their sandwiches in "wraps." You may have seen these the last time you were at the airport—it's like a tortilla but for roast beef. A few dads we know have replaced all the bread in the household with this. Sure, their kids complain, but they'll be thanking him at the next doctor's appointment.

MASTER CLEANSE

There's nothing even to eat! Instead of solid food, you're supposed to drink "juices" made of vegetables that are supposed to "boost your metabolism." I say that if I'm gonna be drinking nothing but vegetable juice, you might as well throw some vodka in there and make me a Bloody Mary, heh.

Did you know: Japanese Macaques will wash and season potatoes in salt water. Talk about a "salternative" diet!

VEGANISM

My daughter is telling me there's one where you can't even eat all the vegetarian stuff? Oh, boy. Apparently the fat and protein in meat and "animal products" can—supposedly—hurt your heart in heavy doses? Jeez. What are you supposed to put on a sandwich, just the lettuce, tomato, and cheese? Oh—not cheese? Can I even have the bread, or is that "gluten" thing not vegan either?

"RAW FOOD"

Now you're saying I can't even cook the food? Too far. I'm a HUMAN, dang it. Everyone knows that food (i.e., meat) is best served charred and blackened from a charcoal grill with a side of A-1. On this "diet," all you can eat is rabbit food, like, I dunno, corn nuts or the garnishes from around your steak. Not recommended!!!

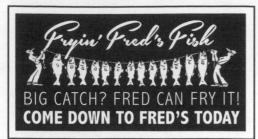
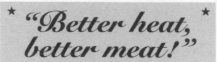

TIPS ON WAITSTAFF

INTERACTION

From the Staff of **DAD MAGAZINE**

It's time to eat out with the family, and you know what that means—captive strangers! There's nothing a dyed-in-the-wool Dad loves more than a fresh audience for his schtick, which is exactly what a good waitstaff provides (along with speedy and cheerful food service). It's the perfect time to test out all your new jokes, to really refine them before the company picnic. Here are a few of our staff's favorites.

"The last time I went out with the family I saw the waiter coming over with the menus, so I cut him off with: 'Is that a menu in your hands or are you just happy to see me?' Everyone was hootin'!"
—*Harry Froelich*

"I tend to go for the classics. When the waitress asks if we want bottled water or tap water, I'll say 'Tap water? I hardly know her!'"
—*Art Parker*

"Wait for the waiter or waitress to introduce themselves by name with 'Hi, I'm ___ and I'll be your server'. Then respond with 'Hi, I'm [YOUR NAME], and I'll be your customer!' It's really funny because I bet they never get that, you know? Totally unexpected."
—*Floyd McAllister.*

"I like to make 'em sweat a little. I'll call one of the waitresses over and look really stern, and say there's a problem. When she asks what the matter is, I'll say 'this food is just too good!' Hah, they love it."
—*John Frangelico*

NOW REMEMBER: With great power comes great responsibility. Sure, we all know your flirting "game" is still top-notch after all these years, but maybe this isn't exactly the time to go overboard. But go ahead and use some of these jokes—and test out some close-up magic tricks while you're at it!

Did you know: 63% of all restaurants are rip-offs

CHOOSING A RESTAURANT

A good way to make sure you're in the driver's seat in terms of choosing where your family eats is… well, driving! Ensure that you're behind the wheel, and you've got the veto on the Chunky Cheese, or wherever your kid wants to go.

WHAT TO ORDER

What's got the most food on it? Restaurants nowadays try to skimp out, but you know better. Make sure you're not doubling up with anyone else at the table, so when you start taking gigantic, unannounced bites of everyone else's food (hey, you're paying), you get to sample as much of the menu as possible.

ETIQUETTE

Try to take in your surroundings. Are there white tablecloths? Maybe stuff the napkin into your collar for that extra little "I'm eating at a fancy restaurant" feeling. Are there license plates and fake taxidermy on the walls? Maybe just make sure you don't get any of the Brand-Name Whiskey Barbecue sauce all over your pleated dockers.

DESSERT

Yes, please!

THE CHECK

Tip well, Dads! See if you can pay without anyone looking. And wink whenever someone asks if anyone's paid. Smoooooth.

WHAT IS THE SPICE OF LIFE?

POINT

VARIETY IS THE SPICE OF LIFE!

by **JEROME DUFFER**

When I think of the way food has changed since I was a kid, my head starts to spin. I grew up in the days of TV dinners, overcooked meatloaf, and tuna noodle casserole. Beige slop! The best we could hope for was a special night out to the Chinese restaurant two towns over, and even that got tiresome. I longed for variety, for flavor!

Now when I walk into the grocery store, a cornucopia of tastes awaits me! My pantry is filled with exotic spices, like tarragon and Old Bay, just waiting to enliven my culinary creations. Want to take a trip to Thailand? Squeeze this Sriracha on your scrambled eggs! And instead of boring apples and peanut butter as an after-school snack, I can feed my kids carrots and hummus all the way from the Middle East! Man, I would have killed for some tahini back in my day. These kids just don't know how good they have it.

Some dads out there are content to eat the same ol' meat and potatoes with salt and pepper every night, but I can't imagine anything more boring. It's a rich world out there, why not experiment? Shop in the "International" food section, buy the "Spanish" rice, and ask the clerk about that quinoa thing! Forget those losers who want to stay in the past—I've got a one-way ticket to a flavorful future.

Science Corner

HOW DOES YOUR TONGUE WORK?

Steakiness

Hoity — Toity

Sour — Bitter

Salty — Sweet

Hoo nelly, that's spicy · Essential greases

MEDLEY CO.

MC

NET WT. 1¼ OZ.

GROUND

ALLSPICE

POWDER

Ingredients - Damn Close to Everything

SPICE COMPANY
CHICAGO, ILLINOIS

MAKES FOOD TASTE GREAT!
TIPS ON BACK

Plain
TABLE
SALT

JUST GOOD OLD-FASHIONED SALT

Iodized

THIS SALT SUPPLIES IODIDE, A NECESSARY NUTRIENT.

NET WT. 26 OZ. (1 LB., 10 OZ.) 737 g

SALT IS THE SPICE OF LIFE!

by **KENNY ERRINGTON**

Good chicken, mashed potatoes, and the occasional green bean is what I was raised on and it did me just fine. You know why? Salt. Old-fashioned table salt, too; none of this fancy Kosher business. Sometimes my dad would bring out the hot sauce on special occasions, but salt is all it takes to keep my food edible and hearty, and I just don't see why we have to complicate things.

I walk into my supermarket and barely know where I am. The deli turkey is slathered in something called "chipotle," they got cheese that comes from a goat, and waffles are all the way from Belgium. And last week I went to a fast food joint only to find them making cheeseburgers with smoked "gouda."

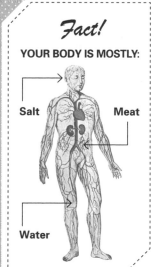

Fact!

YOUR BODY IS MOSTLY:

Salt　　Meat

Water

And you wouldn't believe my kids. It's all "What do you mean you don't know what pH is?" and yapping about something called Nutella, which I finally looked up just to discover it comes from Italy. I don't know where the hell they've been getting this stuff, but I want to remind them that flavored spreads don't grow on trees!

I say if it ain't broke, don't fix it. I want familiarity in my dinners, not trips to foreign countries where they probably make you drive on the wrong side of the road. So you can keep your cappuccinos and your sushi, just leave me a well-salted steak.

MY FIRST GRILL:

A PERSONAL STORY

by **MALCOLM LACRUZ**   Illustration by **LARS LEETARU**

MY FIRST GRILL? It wasn't fancy or expensive. It had no warming rack for buttery buns, no porcelain-enameled grates for easy cleaning, and certainly no built-in thermometer. It was a simpler time, and my grill was little more than a glorified coal-pit, with room for six burgers at a time if you employed my secret space-saving methods. Still, it was my first grill, and dear "Grillver Cleveland" will always hold a place in my heart.

My love for grilling existed long before Grillver came into my life. As a child, I eagerly awaited our neighborhood's block parties, when my parents manned the block-famous kebab stand. Such smells! Such sounds! The marinade sputtering against hot coals, my dad's "If the Grill's Too Hot, You're Too Old!" apron, the neighbors' complaining about how tough the meat was. How I longed to someday take up his mantle.

I moved out of the house at eighteen with a secondhand futon, a duffel bag full of dirty clothes, and my very first grill. It was a red Char-Braille (couldn't afford the brand name!) and I grilled pretty much everything I ate. Burgers, beef stew, spaghetti—you name it, I grilled it. Sometimes I'd pull it next to my bed at night and drape my arm around it, dreaming of the day my future kids would bestow me with my own apron. "Dad's Grillin' So Everyone's Chillin'," maybe.

But the real story here is how Grillver helped me meet the love of my life. The day began like any other. I sprang out of bed at the crack of dawn, ready to face the day. I had a big morning ahead of me, and I was excited to get into the office and sell the heck out of those scientific calculators. Bonus time was barreling down on us all like a freight train, and Malcolm Lacruz was ready. A hearty breakfast is the first step to any hearty sales day, so I threw some sausages on the grill and hopped in the shower. Suddenly, all I could hear was alarms, even over my personal rendition of "Desperado"! I scrambled out of the bathroom and got dressed, still sopping wet, only to find my apartment filled with smoke!

Amidst the smoke I opened my front door to find this tall firefighter guy who immediately threw a blanket over me and rushed me out the front door (all before I fainted in his arms). I'll admit that the encounter left me a little light-headed, and not just from all the oxygen he made me inhale! We went out for beers and pretty much never stopped talking. And now, twelve years later, we're married with two beautiful kids and a grill that fits 32 burgers at a time! And it was all thanks to my first grill.

GAS VS. CHARCOAL: DADS SOUND OFF

JERRY, MILWAUKEE, WI: *"Charcoal all the way! You can't beat that flavor."*

PAT, GLEN ROCK, NJ: *"Gas, baby! That convenience is untouchable."*

JEFF, SHERWOOD, AR: *"Why choose? With this little hybrid system I've worked out, you get the best of both worlds! Sure, I didn't have eyebrows for a few months but: no pain, no gain!"*

MIGUEL, ABIQUIU, NM: *"You aren't a real chef unless you've dug a pit in your backyard, Chief."*

THE ONLY 5 RECIPES YOU NEED TO KNOW

{SERIOUSLY, DON'T LEARN ANY MORE}

by **THE DAD MAGAZINE TEST KITCHEN**   *Photos by* **MICHAEL REALI**

When it comes to providing dinner, dads know that take-out should be left for emergencies only (like that time you tried to clean the oven with ammonia and had to seal off the room for two days). What better way to provide for your family than by showering them with a hearty, creative meal? Of course, not all of us are blessed with creativity in the kitchen, but that doesn't mean cooking should be out of our reach. See what the Dad Magazine Test Kitchen has cooked up for you, and surprise your family tonight!

Fact!

For most of human history, recipes were passed down through an oral tradition. The first recorded instance of a written recipe was found at the ancient Egyptian city of Heliopolis—a set of glyphs engraved on the tomb of a powerful pharaoh describing a process for making sloppy joes. We hope he brought enough for Anubis!

1 MEAT & CHEESE PLATE

see photo shown opposite

If you can shop the cold-cuts aisle, you can have dinner! Slice up some cheddar, fan it out on a plate with hard salami, and serve with crackers for some casual hors d'oeuvres, like they do in Europe!

2 GRILLED STEAK

see photo on page 50

Just put them on the grill, at least 15 minutes per side. You don't want to give your family *E.coli*, do you? Maybe make that 20. But why be picky about what goes on the grill—go with whatever meat ya got. Pork chops, lamb chops, mutton chops . . .

3 BAKED BEANS

see photo on page 51

Pretend you're back in the Navy with this classic dish! Simply dump a can of beans in a baking dish and bake 'em. Dangerous sodium levels? More like dangerous sodi-YUM levels! Ahoy!

4 SPAGHETTI

see photo on page 52

We know this isn't exactly 101, but bear with us! Just buy some meat and cook it. Stir in some tomato sauce and dump it on top of some pasta that you've boiled for either 30 seconds or 20 minutes! Viola! That Boyardee can beat it, there's a new sheriff in town.

5 CHICKEN

see photo on page 53

Just find a chicken and make it. Yeah, however you want! What is this, Le Cirque? Yes, the skin is supposed to be burnt. Wiseass.

Bonus Recipe:
A SALAD

see photo on page 53

Because we know that, realistically, you need more greens in your diet than decorative parsley, so here ya go. Tear apart a head of iceberg lettuce and toss it in a bowl with some carrots, tomatoes, and any other veggies you can stomach. Serve with Thousand Island dressing (not that vinagrette crap).

BEYOND STYLE... A LIFESTYLE

A NEW LINE OF PREMIUM CLOTHING

BROUGHT TO YOU FROM THE FINE FOLKS AT DAD MAGAZINE · AVAILABLE AT ALL FINE STORES

FASHION + GROOMING

BONDING OVER BEARDS

One Dad remembers

59

ARE YOUR DUDS A DUD?

Reinvent your wardrobe

60

PICKING PIPES

Accessorize like the best of us

72

THE COMB-OVER

You are fooling no one by growing one lock of hair super-long and using it to try and cover your bald spot.

INSTEAD:

Take the bull by the horns and just shave it off already. I you aren't ready to go fully shaved, try leaving a short amount of hair on the sides.

THE HIPPY-SCRAGGLE

Still sporting your counter-culturally long mane from the '60s despite the fact that it's thinned out quite a bit? It's time for an update.

INSTEAD:

Buzz your hair short on the sides — leave the front a bit longer and slick it back for a modern-retro look. A handlebar moustache adds quirk.

HAIR-DON'T SOLUTIONS

THE LUNATIC

Though a head and face full of hair is very "in," if you don't keep it under control, you'll look like you belong in a padded cell.

INSTEAD:

Keep the length of your beard, just trim it neatly Cropping hair close to your head will make you look a bit more sane.

THE OVER-DYE

We know you are too old to have jet-black hair with no signs of gray, and even if we didn't, the dye-stains on your skin give it away.

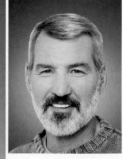

INSTEAD:

Opt for a more natural "salt and pepper" look. Try "Touch of Gray" by Just For Men. Apply moisturizer around your hairline to avoid staining.

THE AU NATURALE
When you prefer to keep things as nature intended.

THE DALI
Announces your artistic nature to the world.

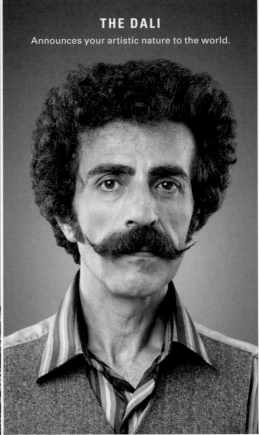

THE IMPERIAL
For the regal man who's master of his domain.

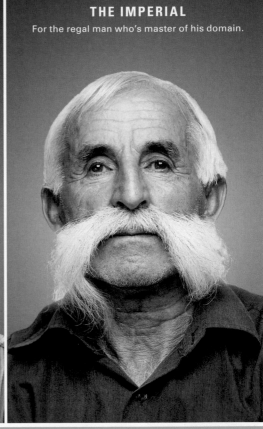

FACIAL HAIR IDEAS

THE CHEVRON
Perfect if you fancy yourself the Tom Selleck type.

THE SANTA CLAUS
Just the right look for a jolly old soul.

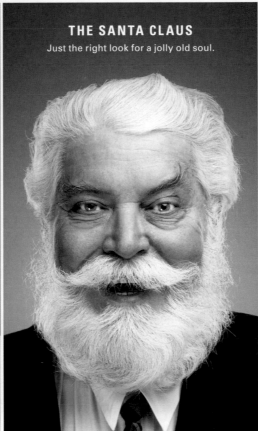

THE CHIN CURTAIN
Keeps the turkey-neck hidden away.

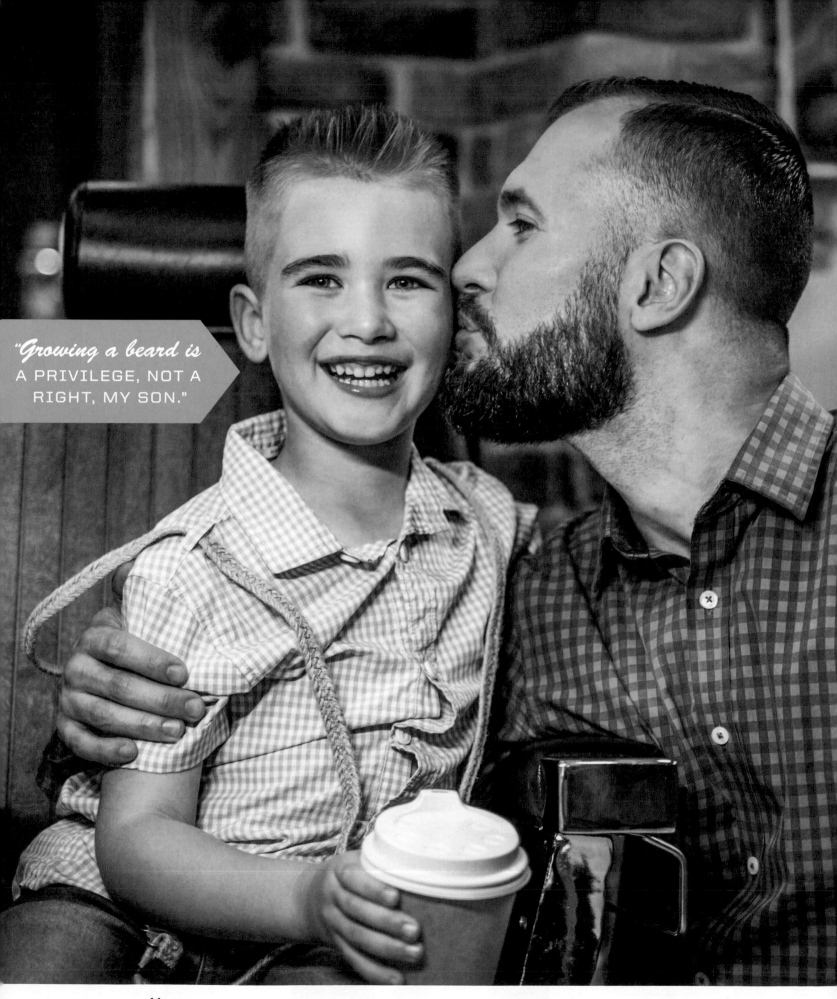

"*Growing a beard is* A PRIVILEGE, NOT A RIGHT, MY SON."

Above: My son Chip and grandson Woody at the barbershop. Soon it will be time for Chip to pass along words of wisdom about growing a beard to his son, much like I did for him when he was a young pup.

HOW TO

TALK TO YOUR SON ABOUT

GROWING A BEARD

by **FLOYD MCALLISTER**   *Photo by* **NEJRON PHOTO**

I was doing some routine maintenance in the attic recently when I came across this letter I wrote some years ago, when my son sprouted his first facial hair. Today I'm proud to say he sports a beautifully maintained beard; and not to toot my own horn, but I believe my words of wisdom steered him in the right direction. We've reprinted it here, for all you Dads out there who may be going through a similar phase with your sons.

"Every man is king of his own beard"

—Persian proverb

DEAR YOUNG SON,

You've grown up so fast. It seems like just yesterday that you were reaching for my hand as we crossed the street, and now you're telling me you can't wait to grow a beard. I'm so proud of you, son, but there are some things I want you to know. Having a beard may sound like fun, but it's a big responsibility. I see young men these days growing them without any thought whatsoever—ingrown hairs across their necks, inconsistent stubble lengths—and my heart sinks. Beards are hard work and deserve respect!

In my day, a man wouldn't dream of growing a full beard until he spent at least ten years with his mustache. I'm not saying things were better then, but it gives you a sense of the beard reverence that's been lost on this generation. When I had my mustache (1983–1990), I had to learn to wake up early to catch the perfect trimming light, and I had remember to carry a comb with me in case of loose hairs. I spent extra time in the shower conditioning my beard, and in the library researching beard-maintenance techniques, knowing someday I'd get to use them. You know what else I learned in that library? Patience, responsibility, and maturity.

Growing a beard is a privilege, not a right, my son. You are lucky to come from hirsute stock—some boys will only dream of growing a beard as thick and full as yours will be. Wear it for them. Wear it for the men with beards in their heart and not on their faces. Wear it for the men with thin mustaches and patchy cheeks. It's true that a beard is an outward symbol of your own pride and comfort in yourself. But it is also a beacon for those who cannot grow such a symbol. Earn this privilege.

Love,
YOUR FATHER

=DAD MAG=
Fashion Guide

DAD RAGS

ARE YOUR DUDS A DUD? IT'S TIME TO CLEAN UP YOUR ACT. LUCKILY WE'RE HERE TO HELP.

Photos by **MICHAEL REALI**

We know what you're thinking: *Fashion, phooey! Who needs it?* But clothes are important—otherwise we'd all be, you know, *naked*. Don't fight it, embrace it. Before you know it, you'll be begging to do your own clothes shopping. This handy guide offers suggestions for all aspects of your life: from the boardroom to the bedroom and all stops in between. No matter whether your collars are blue or white, we've got you covered.

Down and Dirty

{A} Looking this sharp, it's no wonder Chester always shows up for work with a smile. His orange suede welder's jacket (**TILLMAN**) and sand-colored utility work dungarees (**CARHARTT**) are as durable as they are stylish. His western plaid shirt (**FARMALL IH**) and suede shoes (**ROCKWELL**) look as great on the job as they do 'round the house.

{B} Though Rico's wearing denim-on-denim, he smartly avoids looking like he donned a jean-jumpsuit thanks to contrasting shades: light gray for his long- sleeved denim shirt (**LANDS' END**) and a medium wash for his wide-leg jeans (**WRANGLER**).

{C} Louis keeps it classic in plaid flannel (**LANDS' END**) and light-wash blue jeans (**LEE**).

Heavy-duty orange gloves with gray detailing and chocolate-colored workboots (**TIMBERLAND**) protect his extremities.

{D} Leon's not mentally ready for high-waisted dad jeans *quite* yet, so he brazenly sports dark-wash, slim-cut denim (**LEVI'S**). A custom-embroidered name tag adds personality to his standard blue button-down short-sleeved work shirt (**CARHART**).

{E} A non-wrinkle cotton coverall (**DICKIES**) keeps Herb looking crisp all day long, and it's charcoal-gray color helps any grit-n-grime blend right in. A contrasting green handkerchief (**KAISER**) in a festive paisley pattern provides a pop of color.

{F} Marvin favors a color-coordinated ensemble. His yellow polo (**HARBOR BAY**) matches his yellow and brown gloves (**MCR**), which match his yellow company-provided tools and helmet. Complementary navy twill work pants and rugged brown work boots with rubber soles (*both by* **CATERPILLAR**) complete the look.

HARD at WORK

continued:

Buttoned Up

{A} Mark cuts an impressive figure in a sharp gray suit and zingy red tie (**both by JOS. A BANK**).

{B} Otto livens up long days at the office with a playful patterned tie (**JERRY GARCIA**) and a classic two-button suit (**CALVIN KLEIN**).

{C} Miguel looks fit for a king in a dashing royal-blue suit (**KENNETH COLE**) and striped tie (**MACY'S**).

{D} For a more business-casual look, Tony dresses down in flattering black trousers (**TED BAKER LONDON**) and sporty short-sleeve shirt (**UNDER ARMOUR**).

{E} No one loves color combos like Gary, who goes bold with a green-on-green combo tie (**BROOKS BROTHERS**) and top (**J. CREW**).

{F} Anuj shows off a little workday sass in a timeless black suit (**JOS. A BANK**) and preppy plaid necktie (**J. CREW**).

{G} Elmer makes a name for himself with a bold red ID lanyard (**STAPLES**) over a classic checked button-down shirt (**L.L. BEAN**).

Putt Putt

{A} Chester embodies the classic golfing dad in khaki chinos (**DOCKERS**), an official U.S. Open striped polo, and cleated sneakers (**L.L. BEAN**).

{B} Roger's cheerful orange polo (**TOMMY HILFIGER**) and sophisticated charcoal slacks (**BANANA REPUBLIC**) take him straight from the golf course to a night out with the Mrs.— just a quick swap of his white and brown cleats (**HUSH PUPPY**) for dress shoes, of course.

Wheel's Go 'Round

{C} Donald's not afraid to embrace color and is protected from head to ankle in Euro-tinged bike gear (**RABOBANK**) and from ankle to toe in chartreuse cycling shoes (**DIADORA**). His noggin remains safely cradled in a **GIRO** helmet.

{D} Rick's sharp shades (**RUDY**) give his gear some 'tude (*shirt and shorts*, **BREAKAWAY**; *shoes*, **SIRI**).

Fun in the Sun

{E, F, I} Harvey, Gary, and Otto are ready to head straight to Margaritaville in authentic vintage **TOMMY BAHAMA** Hawaiian shirts decorated in festive patterns of tropical orchids, retro cars, and tipsy parrots. Shorts in khaki cargo, olive (*both from* **OLD NAVY**), and buttery yellow linen (**RALPH LAUREN**) keep things relaxed and pair nicely with **CROCS**.

{G} Tony prefers a figure-flattering and athletic look (*shirt and shorts;* **NIKE**; *thongs;* **LANDS' END**).

{H} Garrett brings retro-chic to the poolside in a navy gingham button-down (**J.CREW**), crisp white jeans (**LEVI'S**), and leather boat shoes (**SPERRY**).

{H,I} Otto's Panama Fedora (**STETSON**) and Garret's straw Stingy Brim Fedora (**WORMSER**) keep things dignified, even after a gin and tonic or two.

A

B

Rugged Terrain

{A} While Herb keeps his eyes peeled for the elusive yellow-bellied sapsucker, it's hard to miss how great he looks sporting a long-sleeved button-down (**OUTDOOR LIFE**), roomy extra-wide-leg cargo shorts (**OLD NAVY**), and braided belt (**NAUTICA**). The thin and floppy brim of the birding hat (**SUN TRIPPER**) perched on his head provides sun protection without interfering with binoculars. Breathable hiking shoes (**L.L. BEAN**) keep the tootsies comfy, and a great pair of Argyle socks (**DOCKERS**) add interest to those bird legs.

{B} Albert's gaining traction in his cushioned trail boots (**MERRELL MEN**)—easy on the joints and tough on the terrain. Trekking poles (**REI**) keep him steady on his feet. Wide-waisted cotton shorts (**KIRKLAND SIGNATURE**) are comfy and look great "hiked" up high to reveal a toned mid-thigh.

{C} Lee's perfectly outfitted to bring home the big one this time in premium waders (**ORVIS**) so stylish there's no need to fish for compliments.

{D} Whether you're out for a quiet stroll in the woods or kickin' it up at the corral, Western fashions are always a favorite. Chester cuffs his jeans (**WRANGLER COWBOY CUT**) to show off the detailed embroidery on his authentic cowboy boots (**ACME WESTERN**). A vintage western shirt with pearl buttons and white piping (**ROCKMOUNT RANCH WEAR**) and straw cowboy hat (**RODEO KING**) evoke Roy Rogers in his prime.

Winter Wonderland

{A} When the Mrs. sends Lionel out to shovel the walk, he's fully prepared to do it in comfort and style with his puffer coat (**ELM RIDGE**) and matching scarf and tassle-cap set (*both by* **GAP**). Heavy-duty snow boots (**GOLDEN GOOSE**) keep his feet warm and dry, no matter how deep the snow.

{B} Elmer's ready to take all that winter can toss his way in a red brushed-cotton button-down shirt, beige fleece-lined hooded parka with deep front pockets (*both by* **LANDS' END**), and brown suede galoshes (**L.L. BEAN**). A home-sewn knit cap provides a touch of whimsy.

{C} Miguel keeps warm and fashionable in a cheery periwinkle-blue nylon hooded parka (**COLUMBIA**) and charcoal nylon cargo pants with large velcro-close security pockets (**OLD NAVY**). A royal-blue mock turtleneck (**GAP**) is versatile and never goes out of style. Sensible waterproof black sneakers (**SKETCHERS**) transcend the seasons to remain wearable all year long.

{D} A heavy forest-green courduroy button-down shirt (**L.L. BEAN**) helps keep Harvey warm, while his light-wash high-waisted cargo jeans (**KIRKLAND SIGNATURE**) keep him stylish. A tan faux-suede coat with gathered waist and cuffs (**CLUB ROOM**) keeps the heat in, while brown leather shoes with thick rubber soles (**TIMBERLAND**) keep the cold out.

{E} Raymond's rugged jeans (**LEVI'S**) with rolled cuffs are a perfect complement to his nary brick red courduroy jacket (**EDDIE BAUER**). A versatile brown fleece-lined vest (**MARMOT**) and brown suede boots (**REDWING**) provide the finishing touches to this classic and masculine ensemble.

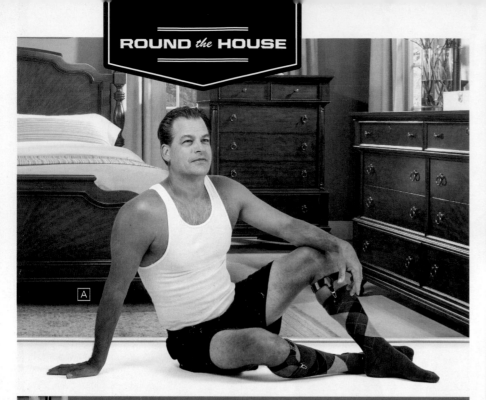

Rise and Shine

It's time to get up, get dressed, and start it all over again.

{A} Underneath it all, Tony's a sensitive guy, so he favors the comfort of silk boxers (**IZOD**) in a deep charcoal gray and sleek Argyle dress socks (**FINE FIT**) in cocoa brown. Sock garters (**LUXURY DESIGN**) hold them in place while keepin' things classy.

{B} Gary's a simple guy and likes simple things, right down to his choice in skivvies: scoop-neck undershirt and tightie-whities (*both by* **FRUIT OF THE LOOM**) all the way.

{C} In the morning, Harvey enjoys puttering around the house in his cozy pinstripe terrycloth bathrobe (**STAFFORD**). Though it's anyone's guess what's beneath the robe, it's a safe bet that he'll be wearing is favorite white crew socks (**HANES**) down below.

{D} Raymond expects the same kind of efficient multi-tasking from his undergarments as he does from his staff at work; his Shirt Stay-Down® with No-slip clips® (**HOLDUP SUSPENDER COMPANY**) keep his shirt perfectly tucked while preventing his socks (**GOLD TOE**) from slipping. He appears all-business on the outside—little do they know he's rockin' polka-dot undershorts (**JOCKEY**).

BITS AND PIECES

Now that we've got you up to speed with the core of your wardrobe, try these add-ons to give all of your parts that final spit-and-polish.

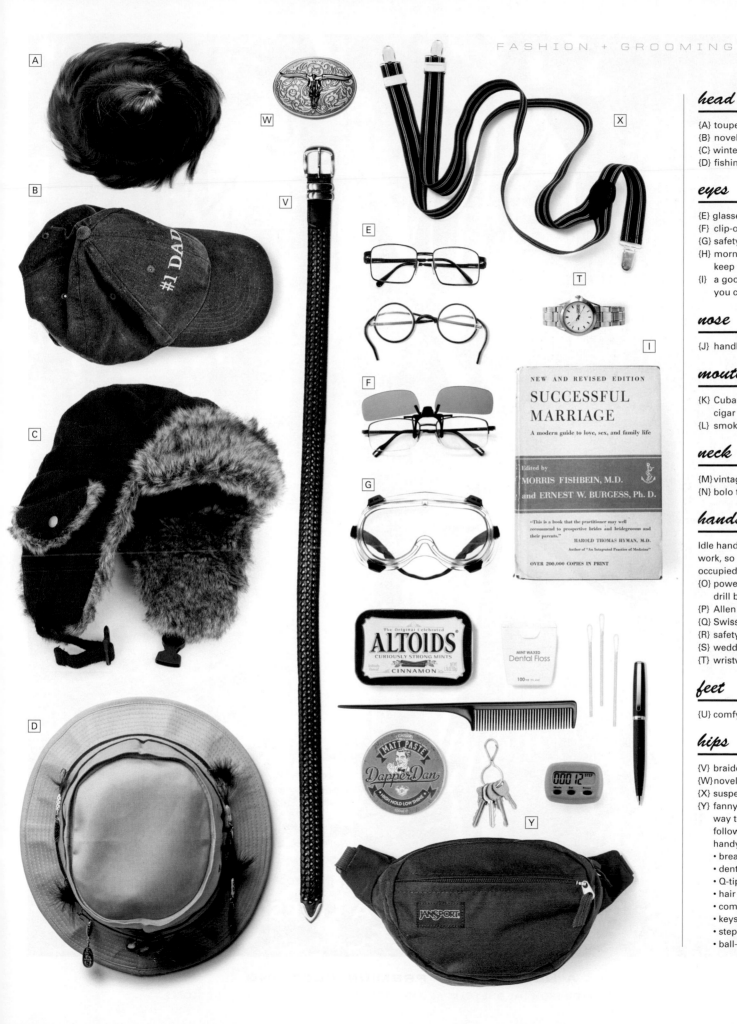

head

{A} toupee (if needed)
{B} novelty ball cap
{C} winter fur cap
{D} fishing hat

eyes

{E} glasses
{F} clip-on sunglasses
{G} safety goggles
{H} morning paper to keep you informed
{I} a good book to keep you cultured

nose

{J} handkerchiefs

mouth

{K} Cuban cigars (with cigar cutter)
{L} smoking pipe

neck

{M} vintage novelty ties
{N} bolo tie

hands

Idle hands are the devil's work, so keep 'em occupied:
{O} power drill with drill bits
{P} Allen keys
{Q} Swiss army knife
{R} safety gloves
{S} wedding band
{T} wristwatch

feet

{U} comfy slippers

hips

{V} braided belt
{W} novelty belt buckle
{X} suspenders
{Y} fannypack—a great way to keep the following items handy:
• breath mints
• dental floss
• Q-tips
• hair cream
• comb
• keys
• step counter
• ball-point pen

BEYOND STYLE... A LIFESTYLE

A NEW LINE OF PREMIUM CLOTHING
BROUGHT TO YOU FROM THE FINE FOLKS AT DAD MAGAZINE · AVAILABLE AT ALL FINE STORES

FEATURE ARTICLES

HAPPY BIRTHDAY DAD!

A look back at an illustrious century of paternal journalism

76

LACKING VISION?

Dads around the country are losing their glasses—meet the dad who saw the truth

84

A DANGEROUS READ

The thrilling latest in Dad Fiction from author Jim Hopper

87

100 YEARS

OF DAD MAGAZINE

...IN COVERS!

DAD MAGAZINE sure has come a long way from our humble beginnings. The name may have changed, but our spirit has stayed the same. We're proud of our roots, and in the following pages you can see just how much we've grown.

OPPOSITE

The very first issue of our magazine,
then called *Father's Discussion Monthly*.

April 1916 • 20 cents

20 cents

April 1916

Fathers Discussion
Monthly

"Papa, Can You Hear
the Great Apes?"
— E.R. Burroughs

"A Father
Discusses the
Great
War With
His Daughter
and Son"
from Arthur C. Doyle

"A Lively Collection Of Fathering Tales"

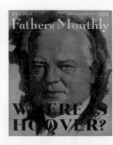

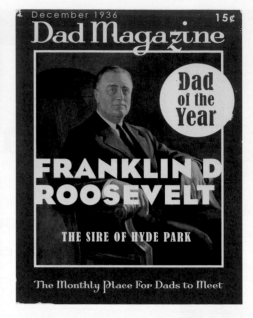

OCTOBER 1926 • 25 cents

June 1927 • 25 cents

December 1928 • 25 cents

September 1930 • 15 cents

May 1933 • 15 cents

DECEMBER 1936 • 15 cents

October 1938 • 15 cents

November 1939 • 15 cents

October 1941 • 25 cents

October 1942 • 25 cents

February 1945 • 25 cents

JULY 1946 • 25 cents

May 1949 • 25 cents

December 1950 • 25 cents

May 1951 • 25 cents

August 1953 • 25 cents

September 1954 • 25 cents

NOVEMBER 1955 • 25 cents

November 1959 • 25 cents

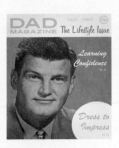
November 1960 • 30 cents

May 1964 • 30 cents

November 1967 • 75 cents

NOVEMBER 1967 • 1 dollar

FEBRUARY 1976 • $2.50

November 1972 • 1 dollar

September 1975 • 1 dollar

February 1978 • $2.50

May 1981 • $3.75

June 1987 • $3.75

August 1988 • $3.75

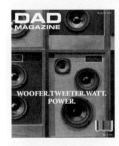
March 1989 • $3.75

July 1991 • $3.75

AUGUST 2006 • $6.99

May 1996 • $3.75

November 1999 • $3.75

January 2000 • $4.99

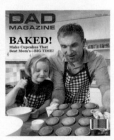
March 2002 • $4.99

July 2010 • $6.99

December 2014 • 6.99

OUR DAD
CENTURY

(above) Our "founding father," Hans Frölich.

HOW *DAD MAGAZINE* GREW FROM A TWINKLE IN ITS FATHER'S EYE TO THE GRAND POPPA OF GENERAL-INTEREST PERI-DAD-ICALS

NE HUNDRED YEARS. A century. The time has really flown, right? To me, the story of *Dad Magazine* is the story of America. Hard work, collaboration, and innovation have led us through the decades—and let's face it, we don't look too shabby for 100! Though does it look like I'm losing my hair? I feel like it's getting thinner. Hold on, I gotta check this out.

Okay, to tell the story of *Dad Magazine*, we need to tell the story of our "founding father," Hans Frölich. Hans was born in New York City in 1870, the second son of German immigrants who fled the revolutions of 1848, searching for a new world in which to start a family. Hans always spoke fondly of his father. "He gave me my love for the written word," he wrote in his autobiography, *A Father's Journey*, "and my sense of discovery. It's is because of him that I will never stop futzing with this blasted automobile."

However, Hans's parents would never see all that their son would accomplish in his life. They died just before his twelfth birthday, forcing Hans onto the streets in order to support himself and his siblings. He and his brother Henrick soon found work as newsies, hawking papers up and down Manhattan for pennies, sticking to a work ethic we wish we could teach our kids. He also had an ear for the scandalous, reporting interesting tidbits of gossip back to the papers. The *Mail* and *Express* eventually realized he should be off the streets and in the bullpen, and he was hired as a reporter in 1888.

Hans (who went by the nickname "Jack" in his professional work) gained a reputation as a savvy and cutthroat journalist, always on the pulse. Readers couldn't get enough of the scandals and sensations he'd uncover, no matter how nutty. Few could forget his famous reportage during the 1890s infamous Sack Coat Shortage fiasco. However, close readers will notice that he kept dads on his mind in all his writing. "I always attempted to illuminate how the stories of the day affected the fathers," He wrote. "Whether it was the lousy season the Yankees were having or how to find a decent beer to drink in peace during Prohibition."

Soon enough, he had his own potential fatherhood on his mind. He had married Francine Warner, a secretary at the newspaper, in 1894, and the two desperately wanted a family. In 1896, Milton Warner came along, with Clara Ann following soon after.

Hans's career flourished and his children grew, and as they neared adulthood

"WHAT ABOUT FATHERS? WHERE SHALL THEIR VOICES LIVE, SO THAT OTHERS MAY SEE THE LIGHT THEY BRING THE WORLD?"

he began to long for something more than the gossip and sensationalism upon which he had built his career. It just happened to be a time of upheaval for the magazine industry—*National Geographic* was founded in 1899, and *Photoplay* in 1912, introducing many readers to the stories and images from around the globe. Those stories and images were often of war and destruction. In contrast, Hans had a vision for a magazine that would stand in relief to the turmoil, a collection of stories about fathers that would provide a positive alternative to the horrors of war. "What about fathers?" he wrote to his brother in 1914. "Where shall their voices live, so that others may see the light they bring the world?"

Hans used every connection he had, and on April 10, 1916, the first issue of *Fathers Discussion Monthly* was printed. Fun Fact: The first copyeditor was the third cousin of Henry Luce, founder of *Time!* Anyway, *Fathers Discussion Monthly* originally ran uplifting fiction stories on and around the themes of fatherhood, and it became a haven for writers whose paternal writing instincts had been shut out of the literary world. For instance, it was there that L. Frank Baum published *The Father of Oz*, and where J. M. Barrie published Peter Pan's oft-forgotten sequel, *The Boy Who Finally Grew Up after a Sound Talking To*.

The magazine quickly found its niche, reaching a wide array of fatherly readers in the Northeast. In 1926, it went through its first metamorphosis with the hiring of editor Joseph Hadden. The magazine industry was at a turning point, with the nation's dads increasingly turning to radio and moving pictures for entertainment, and Hadden saw that changes had to be made for the magazine to thrive far into the future. He was also concerned that the literary tone served only a higher class of fathers. "I want to reach the Everyman Dad," he wrote in a memo to Froelich. "I want Dads across the country to turn to us for support, guidance, and tips on how to clean their gutters."

It was under Hadden's watch that the magazine expanded to non-fiction reporting. He also spearheaded a campaign for national distribution, utilizing movie theaters and radio programs to encourage Dads around the country to ask their local drugstores to stock their favorite monthly. Finally, he knew the time had come for a snappier name. *Fathers Discussion Monthly* became *Fathers Monthly* in 1926, and by 1929 its name changed to *Dad Magazine*.

It's 1929, betcha know what comes next! That's right—prosperity! Despite the rest of the world being in a bit of a

"Our Dad Century" continued on page 124

PROFILES IN DAD COURAGE:

HERO DAD
GETS QUIET TIME

THE STORY OF ONE MAN WHO WADED THROUGH
THE CHAOS TO READ THE DAMN PAPER IN PEACE

by **CLINT HARDLAM**   *Photo by* **LJUPCO SMOKOVSKI**

I T'S SUNDAY MORNING and Wallace Nevins has found peace. Sitting on his front porch in Nicholasville, Kentucky, he nurses a mug of black coffee emblazoned with a witty motto ("It's not a bald spot, it's a solar panel for a sex machine") while reading the Auto Classifieds in the local paper. From the outside he may look like any other dad, but for Nevins, this quiet time is hard won.

Nevins is one of the growing number of stay-at-home dads, the self-described "man-ager" of six kids between the ages of 3 and 14. His wife, Tricia Coleman, is an Economics professor at the nearby University of Kentucky. "When Trish first got pregnant, she was worried she'd have to give up her career. But to be honest I never much cared for being a computer programmer." Yet as Nevins soon learned, full-time parenting is no easy task, and it got harder as the kids kept coming. During an average week, he's tasked with getting five of his children to their schools, then coordinating pick-up

"Hero Dad" continued on page 124

Loud noises can damage your hearing and rattle your brain. Are you exposing yourself to danger? Here are the average decibel levels of everyday household noises.

10 VERY FAINT:
Anyone saying "Dad"; your own sneeze (despite what everyone else says)

30 FAINT:
The TV when someone else is talking and you're trying to hear it

50 MODERATE:
Conversational speech, good music

70 LOUD:
Bad music

90 VERY LOUD:
Someone changing the thermostat; the fridge motor making that noise again

110 DEAFENING:
Anyone practicing an instrument

A LACK OF VISION

ACROSS THE COUNTRY, ALL SIGNS POINT TO A CRIME WAVE TARGETING DADS. SO WHY ISN'T THE GOVERNMENT DOING ANYTHING?

by OLIVER GIBSON, DAD REPORTER

"TO BE HONEST, I can't remember the first time I noticed my glasses were gone," said Clark Jefferson. He's sitting with his wife at the kitchen table of their Durham, NC, home, which they share with three kids. Jefferson is a stocky man, his red polar fleece pullover clinging to a chest that hints of athleticism. Their house is typical, small and on a quiet street, tucked away in a subdivision near the Research Triangle office park. Not the place you'd expect the spark for a national firestorm. "They just weren't anywhere, you know?" he says as he looks up from his hands, squinting to focus on my face. "Something just didn't feel right."

You've likely heard of Clark Jefferson by now. If you haven't, he's the founder of FOCUS—Fathers Opposing Criminal Uprooting of Spectacles, the first organization dedicated to the oft-neglected crime wave sweeping the nation. He's also at the forefront of a massive battle against government corruption, which has him butting heads with the FBI. Quite a lot for this amateur mountain biker.

According to preliminary data gathered from FOCUS's website, at least 21,000 pairs of glasses have gone missing from American households in the past year. That may seem like a case of the ol' forgetfuls, but of those pairs, 73% belonged to dads. "It's a clear case of ongoing crimes targeted against dads, and it's getting worse," says Jefferson.

FOCUS came into, well, focus about a year ago, when Jefferson was speaking to neighbor, and now vice-president, Gary Michaels at a backyard BBQ about his glasses disappearing right from under his nose. "He told me he hadn't been able to find his reading glasses in a week," said Jefferson. He spoke to his wife, Anita, about it that night, and she assured him that Michaels must have just misplaced them." But something didn't feel right to Jefferson.

"I remember the day after that party, Clark told me to ask around to other dads at my office about any cases of missing glasses," said Michaels, an HR administrator at Duke University. Jefferson did the same at IBM, where he works as a software engineer. What they began to discover was a staggering pattern of dads whose glasses seemingly disappeared, and whose concerns were just as easily dismissed.

Anita Jefferson was originally one of the nonbelievers; she admitted to assuming her husband had lost his glasses. "I lose my glasses all the time," she said, "it just didn't seem like a big deal, until he started showing me the stuff all these dads were posting." By that point Jefferson and the half dozen dads he had gathered to his cause had formed an online

CRIME WAVES IN HISTORY TARGETED AT DADS

At the time, many of these incidences were dismissed as Dad Forgetfulness (a condition no longer recognized by the American Psychiatric Association's DSM-5), modern research shows these historic events were potentially crime waves as well.

1639, France
A letter from a court attendant of Louis XIII to a family member details "Le roi ne peut trouver ses chaussures à talons hauts" ("The King, he cannot find his high-heeled shoes")

1905, England
News of the World reports that tweed shooting jackets disappear en masse

1938, America
The Great Watch Misplacement sweeps the Midwest

1981, America
Where the heck is the clicker?

community to encourage dads across the country. As it turned out, they had many, sharing their grievances on FOCUS-DADS.biz's message boards.

"One of the things we started to tap into was the feeling that these dads weren't being taken seriously," said Jefferson. "Here they were, clearly saying 'Well, I left them in the glove compartment and when I came back to the car they were gone' or 'I put them on my nightstand every night and one morning they weren't there,' and they were just being laughed at." But the numbers don't lie, and more dads are coming forward every day.

—

FOCUS has been up and running for almost a year, but soon after he began collecting these stories, Clark Jefferson realized he needed to take action. So he did what any reasonable victim of "petty" crime would do—he went to his local police station to report it. However, instead of the upstanding officers of the law he'd assume were there to help him, he was met with the same derision, suspicion and outright disrespect he'd encountered so many times elsewhere. "They just chuckled to themselves and told me to go home," he said. "They said that even if my glasses were stolen, it's just not worth their time, that I can pick up another pair at the Walgreens on my way home. I don't know if they know this, but glasses are expensive! Besides, I liked my pair. It's a matter of principle." Jefferson tried to contact officers at other precincts in the following days, but none wanted to take up the case.

When asked for comment, Durham Police Spokeswoman Ginny Flint told *Dad Magazine*, "That particular citizen seemed to have an issue where he would often misplace his glasses, and we're dealing with someone with paranoid delusions, frankly. We've tried to handle the situation delicately in the past, but it's proving increasingly impossible." However, it seems they have no proof that these are either delusions or a

"Lack of Vision" continued on page 125

Rebuffed at every turn from traditional law enforcement, FOCUS hired a freelance police sketch artist to create eyewitness images of potential suspects. These and others can be seen on FOCUS's website: FOCUS-DADS.biz.

POLL

DO YOU THINK THE READING-GLASSES CRIME WAVE IS SOMETHING TO WORRY ABOUT?

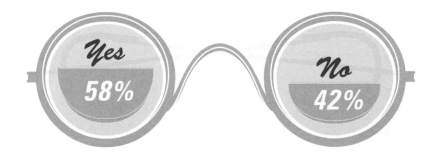

Yes 58% *No* 42%

DAD MAGAZINE BOOK CLUB:

The Father of Danger

Every month, Dad Magazine gives you sneak peeks of the latest in Dad Fiction. This month we have the honor of bringing you the first look at award-winning author Jim Hopper's upcoming thriller, _The Father of Danger_.

Illustration by **PATRICK FARICY**

CARL ANDERSON'S COSTCO-BRAND sneakers made barely any sound as he stood with his back to the idyllic ranch home on the Cul-De-Sac at the end of Franklin Street. *Just get to the house before anyone notices you're gone,* he thought, *and hopefully you won't have to run for it.* He cracked a smile as he continued on, knowing he would not have had the stamina for such a chase if he hadn't kept in shape.

He inched along the wall, gun in hand, replaying the details in his head. A minute ago he had been flipping through his mail, wondering if this invitation to play in some charity softball game next month all the way in Washington, DC, meant that someone had finally noticed his three-year streak as MVP of the local slow-pitch league, when the phone rang.

"Carl," said a breathless, husky voice on the other end. "It's me, Ruby De Ville. Your neighbor," she prompted, when Carl didn't answer.

Carl stood up a little straighter. This Ms. De Ville character was bad news, at least to hear his wife tell it. Moved in down the street out of the blue just a few weeks ago, without so much as a U-Haul.

"I've told you before, Ms. De Ville," Carl said. "I'm a married man. Go borrow a cup of sugar from someone else."

"Please, Carl." Her voice got huskier and even more breathless. "Listen to me. You're in danger. Someone's trying to kill you."

Carl didn't understand at first. Who could possibly be trying to kill him? He worked hard to be a good member of his community, helping with parking during the church fairs and giving his neighbors tips on their leaf-raking techniques.

"They brought me in hoping to seduce you, but since it didn't work they—*get away from me, you brute!* I'll—*help!*"

An ear-piercing scream blared from the phone.

"Ms. De Ville?" Carl said. "Ruby?"

The line crackled. "Help . . . trapped . . . for God's sake, they've got a *bomb*!"

With that, the line went dead. And Carl had realized that if he didn't act quickly, Ruby De Ville would be, too.

The sound of shattering glass jolted Carl back to reality, and he whipped around just in time to see his own windows shattered, two doors down. That dang kid! He had just replaced those. Double-pane, low-E glass! He had of course *wanted* to use hand-made frames, none of that prefab foreign stuff, but who has the time nowadays? Before he knew it, he was on his way to the darn Lowe's to pick up the—oh! Right. It didn't look like Philip or Holly running from the broken window; this guy was clad in a trench coat and a Panama hat, which Carl could never quite believe had gone out of style. It was such a classic look! Bogart knew what he was talking about.

Now was not the time for reminiscing, however. Ruby De Ville was in danger, and Carl would have to save her, even if it meant doing some explaining to the wife later. Shaking his head, Carl cocked his gun, ducked around the corner, and dashed into the alley between his house and that lousy Cal Wheatley's. He ran until his feet went numb in his trusty Air Jorgans, but just as he was approaching Ruby's front door, the cell-phone clip fastened to his Dockers vibrated. He flipped open his phone and raised it to his ear, hoping it was some answers.

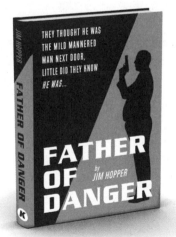

THEY THOUGHT HE WAS THE MILD MANNERED MAN NEXT DOOR, LITTLE DID THEY KNOW HE WAS...

JIM HOPPER

FATHER OF DANGER

FATHER OF DANGER
by JIM HOPPER

"Father of Danger" continued on page 136

HOME + LIFE

GET OFF MY LAWN!

What we're keeping off this month.

90

GARY'S GARDEN

America's second favorite horticulturalist is back with great garden tips.

91

YOUR FAVORITE ROUTES

The results are in! Check out our best ways to make great time.

98

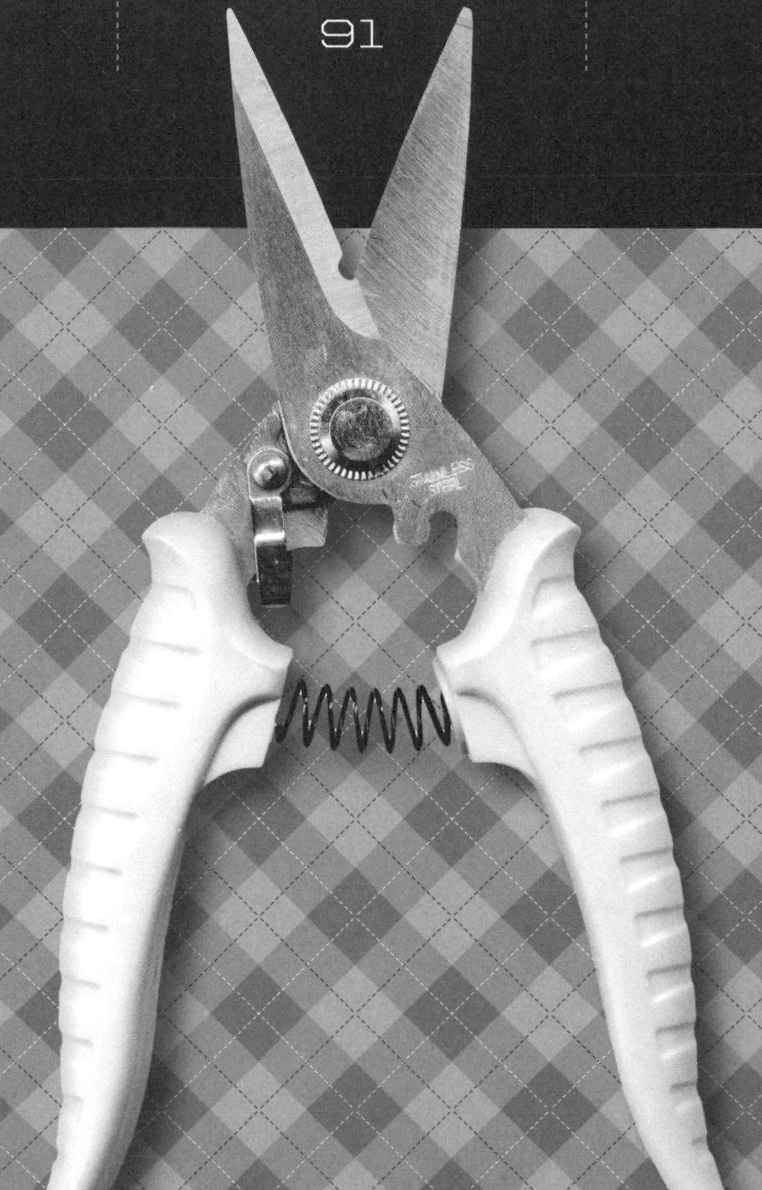

GET THESE THINGS OFF YOUR LAWN!

A DAD IS SURELY THE KING OF HIS LAWN. But did you know that you are under siege as we speak? Threats bearing down on your little fiefdom, plotting to ruin the tiny paradise you've built for yourself. No longer! Here's a run-down of invaders you should watch out for and keep off YOUR lawn.

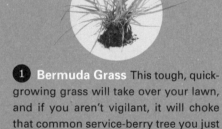

1 Bermuda Grass This tough, quick-growing grass will take over your lawn, and if you aren't vigilant, it will choke that common service-berry tree you just planted to attract the wood thrushes.

2 Dandelion This plant will try to convince you it's a beautiful yellow flower, but don't be fooled! These suckers will pop up in every crevice, attracting deer. Rip up by roots. Best done by small hands. (Your children's hands. Builds character.)

3 Trash This can especially be a problem if you live on a well-trafficked road. Don't let your neighbors toss their garbage onto your lawn. Erect a sign that says it's not a landfill! Or maybe set up shop on your porch and stare 'em all down. That will make any potential litterers think twice, for sure!

4 Strange Dogs A dog is a man's best friend, but a stranger's dog is an agent of chaos. There he is, tearing up your herb garden as we speak! Get that pest out of there before he does some real damage! A fun DIY project would be to make some homemade traps. A strange dog might as well be a deer. Yeah, I went there.

5 Toys Your darn kid is leaving his tricycle on the lawn again. Seems innocuous, sure. But you know what that means? Dead spots. Dead spots all over because he couldn't bring the thing back into the garage. Get it off your lawn and into the community center donation bin! Kid's gotta learn.

6 College Kids Constant vigilance, Dads! Or else you could be overwhelmed with some sophomore philosophy majors lounging around your perfectly trimmed Ryegrass lawn like it was the quad at Loafers University! Better chase these dummies out while you have the chance.

GARY GARY, QUITE CONTRARY

HOW DOES YOUR GARDEN GROW?

by **GARY "GREENTHUMB" GOTTILEB**

Hi Gary,
I've got a nice little garden if I do say so myself, but I'm encountering some serious Blackspot on my roses!
Help!
Fungal in Fort Lauderdale

Fungus, eh? This one's easy! Try spraying your roses with a fungicide every 7–10 days and you should be in great shape! Florida, right? I like it there. Very aggressive wildlife management program.

Dear Gary,
I've got a nice little organic garden that I'm very proud of, but aphids are wreaking total HAVOC on my tomatoes! I don't want to do pesticides, so I'm totally stuck.
Bugged out in Bloomington

Gary!
I've spent a lot of time on my little garden (I'm very proud of it!) but it keeps getting destroyed at night by deer! What the heck do I do?
Desperate in Deerfield

Well, you've really tapped in to something here. The intensity with which I love gardening, I also loathe your common suburban deer. The white-hot intensity of a thousand, thousand suns, Desperate! One day, when I'm in charge, I'll devote government resources to eradicate the Deer Menace. We will hunt them down and destroy every buck, doe, and fawn that dare sully the earth beneath each of their disgusting hooves. The survivors will know fear.

Until then, have you tried a deer fence? They're affordable and easy to install! Should do the trick.

Hey Gary!
I've got a great house and I'm proud of my nice little garden but a new development just went in and I suddenly find myself stuck with a garden in partial shade. I'm having a tough time coaxing my leafy pals out of the ground. Do you have any pointers on how to deal with this?
Darkened in Dayton

Sorry to hear that, Darkened! It's so odd, you know? I try so hard to get my garden to grow at even a snail's pace (not to mention the snails eating all my cucumbers!), but take ONE look out at the forest around Gottileb Estates (my little name for our split-level) and what do you see? Acre after acre of unkempt rampant growth! What gives? My garden is way better than that dumb forest. A KNOWN SHELTER, by the way, of Garyland Enemy Number One: DEER. One day I'm gonna hit that stupid forest with a cleansing fire, and then where will those deer hide? Nowhere!

Anyways, plant some ferns.

That's a tough spot you're in, reader! I would normally suggest a whole SLEW of chemicals, but I appreciate your concern for Mother Earth. Personally, I don't care much for the wild—too unpredictable if you ask me.

Anyways, to keep things organic, try introducing some predators into the environment. Your local gardening supply should have praying mantises or lacewings available. Release 'em near your ta matas and let 'em get to work!

GARY'S TIP OF THE MONTH!

Watch out for seed catalog scams! These bozos will take you for all you're worth if you're not careful. Most assume your average gardener doesn't know the difference between Clynoglossom and Calendula. Before ordering any seeds, call up the company and ask for a thorough rundown of their pricing policies. And if they stop sending you catalogs out of frustration, heck, there are plenty of others out there!

WHAT'S GOING ON WITH

YOUR NEIGHBOR'S YARD?

The neighbors thought the hedges were just getting a bit shaggy. What they discovered was much, much worse.

by **FLOYD MCALLISTER** *Additional reporting by* **GARY GOTTILEB**

Illustration by **SCOTTY REIFSNYDER**

JUST DRIVING BY Woodlawn Terrace in Waterbury, Connecticut, seems like your average street in the New England suburbs. Nicknamed the "Brass City" for its history of manufacturing watches, it's filled with old trees, historic houses, and many verdant lawns. But according to local resident Jeff Washington, one Woodlawner's lawn is not what it seems. Recently, he informed us of some interesting developments in the front yard of the Petersen house. At Dad Magazine, our mission is to keep you informed about what's going on in your life, so we decided to take a closer look.

"It's quite an interesting development, one I've come across rarely in my research, and I'm eager to study it deeper," says Dr. Matthew Holt, who holds a PhD in Yard Science and is the Senior Shrubbery Fellow at Harvard Lawn School (lawn.harvard.edu). "It appears the Petersens'

yard is in what we call a topiatric flux." In layman's terms, topiatric flux is the liminal state between a yard's transformation from your average suburban lawn into a European-style topiary garden, in which hedges are trimmed and clipped into living ornamental statues. Certainly an uncommon occurrence in suburban America.

The topiary arts have been practiced around the world, from Japanese Niwaki to the decoration of Roman atriums. Many English dads embraced the art in the late 1800s as a Jacobethan revival swept the country, but that doesn't explain the development in Waterbury. "I just can't make heads or tails of it," admits Washington, who brought up the issue in the latest school board meeting. "It definitely got the town talking," he said. "Everyone's feeling a bit confused."

Local bookstore owner Maddie Frederickson reports that Mr. Petersen had or-

dered a copy of *Topiary: Garden Craftsmanship in Yew and Box* by Nathaniel Lloyd two weeks before the lawn developments appeared. When asked about the purchase, Dr. Holt says it is possible that Mr. Petersen developed a taste for English cottage garden revival, but it's more likely inspired by the family's recent vacation. "My working theory is that this was spurred by the Peter- sens' trip to Disney Land over their children's spring break." He explains: "Topiary fell out of favor in England in the 18th Century, but American-style topiary was introduced almost entirely by Walt Disney. It's one of the few places in the country to see it."

However, it's no surprise that, given any location for this topiatric flux to take place, it would happen in Connecticut. Topiary arts are most successful with evergreen trees featuring either small leaves or needles, which are abundant in the American Northeast. The famous

Walter Hunnewell Arboretum in Wellesley, Massachusetts, is a mere 118 miles from Waterbury. The Petersens may very well have been inspired in California, but there's no shortage of encouragement to be found on the East Coast.

Traditionally a lawn in topiatric flux exhibits three distinct stages. The first stage, Planting, is evidenced by a sudden uptick in dense evergreen plants on the property. According to our research, the Petersens are currently in the second stage, Shaping, in which these plants are meticulously trimmed to resemble a number of different shapes or creatures. This stage can last anywhere from one to eight months, depending on the Petersens' professional schedules and their willingness to put their kids to work. Which means that the final stage, Maintenance, certainly the most difficult, is fast approaching.

"Topiary requires meticulous attention, something I suspect the Petersens' may not be able to keep up with, given Mr. Petersen's weekly HAM radio club," says Dr. Holt. However, this isn't the Petersens first foray into controversial lawn behavior. Locals still speak in whispers about the Great Hedge Incident of 2003, praying that the next generation will never learn of such suffering. "I'll never forget it," says one

> # "I'll never forget it," says one neighbor…. "First the hedges were so high you couldn't see down the street. Then, the blight came."

neighbor, who wished to remain anonymous. "First the hedges were so high you couldn't see down the street. Then the blight came. Man just wasn't meant for such horticultural feats."

This neighbor also claims that he has attempted to speak to the Petersens multiple times about the impact their lawn could have on the community, but they seem disinterested in the possible ramifications, almost to the point of being hostile. "You know what Mr. Petersen told me when I said these monstrosities could block the sunlight my azaleas so desperately need? He told

me to move them somewhere else!," he said. The Petersens have since failed to return his phone calls, though they have trimmed that topiary down a foot.

Unfortunately, there's not much locals can do but voice their concerns. Many counties have laws on the books regarding basic lawn maintenance to protect residents from fire hazards or cosmetic issues. Waterbury's municipality has no such rules for private property, so the Petersens are free to continue their unorthodox practices. However, one town alderman and dad thinks it's high time Waterbury added some of these ordinances. "You start with topiary, but who knows where it could go from there," she said. "What next, arborcture?"

The bright side, according to Dr. Holt, is that this could be the basis for unprecedented research in the field of Yard Science. "There's no limit to what we can learn about what the heck is going on with the Petersens' yard," he says, and he's encouraging the Petersens' neighbors to keep a close eye and report any new developments. For Mr. Washington, Dr. Holt's enthusiasm is hard to match. "I just don't understand it. Who wants a tree shaped like a dang bear when you can wake up and look out on a beautiful carpet of greenery?" The Petersens could not be reached for comment.

BIGGEST LAWN MISHAPS IN HISTORY

1st Century AD, Babylon
Hanging Gardens of Babylon destroyed from overwatering

1760 BCE, Mesopotamia
Hammurabi's hydrangeas discovered to be luckluster due to poor pH balance

1682, France
Great Versailles Gardens constructed (too precise if you ask us)

1842, Scotland
Great Peat Fire of 1842

1888, London
Botany Ripper terrorized London by slashing all of its major rose gardens; to this day still has not been caught

1962, Kentucky
That time Carl's lawnmower ran amok

THESE SMOKE DETECTORS ARE TOO DAMN SENSITIVE,

IF YOU ASK ME

by **CLINT HARDLAM**

I USED TO BELIEVE that no home should be without a smoke detector. (Really, no home should be without a carbon monoxide detector, radon detector, magnesium detector, or bear detector, but that's for another day.) However, I've recently noticed my home's smoke detector exhibits a certain quickness to react. When did these things get so darned sensitive?

I first noticed this glitch as I was making pancakes one weekend with my daughter. I got a bit distracted explaining how generic-brand pancake mix is just as good as the fancy stuff, and suddenly the pancakes were burnt to a crisp and the smoke detector was ringing loud enough to wake the dead! I immediately turned around and grabbed the jug of orange juice we were going to have with breakfast and emptied it onto the stove to kill the flames. But that contraption just wouldn't shut up until I got up there and took out the batteries.

Smoke detectors need to be programmed to operate in an optimal space. If your house has filled with smoke, there's no need for them to go off. You've already figured out the place is on fire, and you don't want that racket added on top of your stress. When the time comes and the big fire does happen, I'm gonna be too busy mentally checking off all the things on my mental Fire Checklist and doing the important work of saving my family to be distracted by some dang machine. How am I supposed to locate my meticulously packed fire go-bag and put the cat somewhere it can't escape with that infernal noise? You tell ME, First Alert Company of Aurora, Illinois.

And another thing! If I'm sitting right here in the kitchen, why can't the smoke detector see that? I clearly have a handle on the situation if I'm smoking ribs in the oven, or have a stir fry going, or am searing that steak. This is not some crisis! If I walk away for half an hour to do some light weeding, the smoke alarm does not need to tell me what's happening. My internal smoke clock is finely tuned.

Perhaps the time has come for us Dads to stand up and be the smoke detectors we wish to see in the world. Forget the plastic prisons of years past, the endless battery checks and wiring concerns. Learn to detect smoke without the aid of technology. Who runs the world? Dads!

WHAT TO DO IF YOUR FIRE ALARM GOES OFF

- Loudly complain to your family.
- Immediately rush toward it, even if there's smoke in the way.
- Wave a towel at it and grumble to yourself.
- Remove the batteries.
- Whatever you do, don't call the fire department.

PACK YOUR TRUNK

by **FLOYD MCALLISTER**

1. Place heavier things on the bottom to ensure structural integrity.

2. Keep an eye out for efficiency-killing redundancies. Why does everyone need their own towel? Come on, we're family.

3. The keystone of the car pack, located at the center, should always be your densest item. An effective pack will exert a lot of pressure.

4. Put things you don't want people to use in the car towards the bottom. Repeat after me: "Oh, you'll just have to wait until we get there!"

5. Utilize your car's roof rack for oddly shaped items: bikes, skis, those boogie boards you bought the kids and they're probably gonna use this time.

6. Buttress flimsier items with rigid frameworks.

7. Stack your roof rack as high as possible to assert dominance over the other drivers!

8. When purchasing a car, look for a trunk with straight edges to avoid bothersome empty spots.

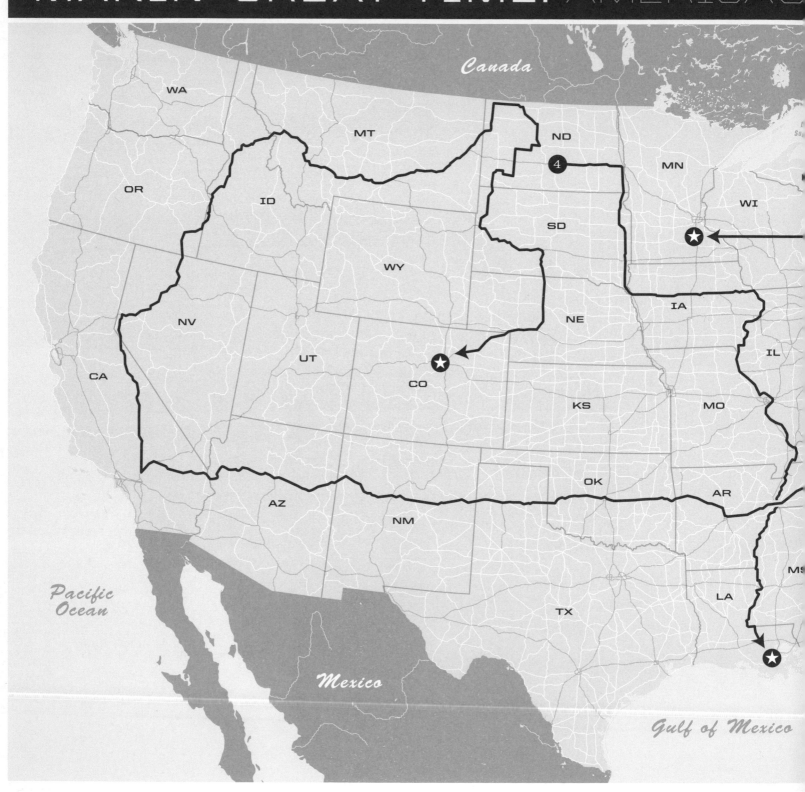

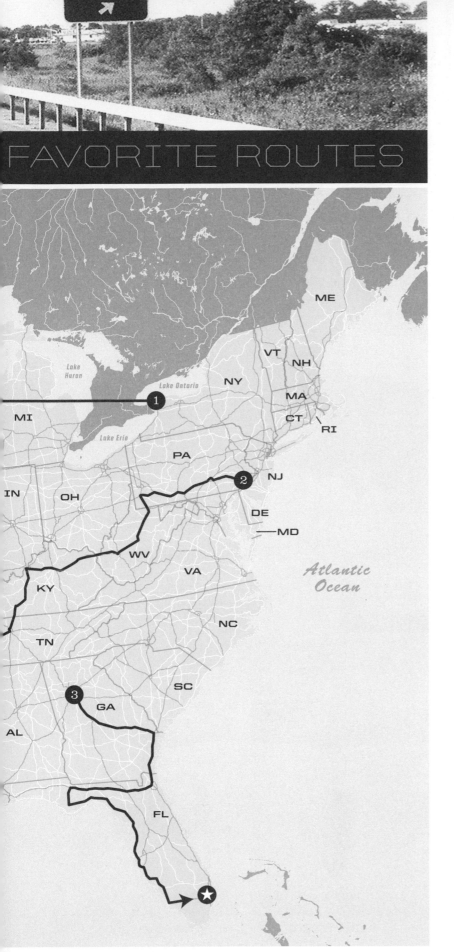

FAVORITE ROUTES

We asked America's Dads for their favorite routes and YOU voted. Here are your winners!

BUFFALO TO ST. PAUL
PAT M. • CRESTED BUTTE, CO
MILES: 732
TIME: 3.5 HOURS, IF YOU DO IT RIGHT

ROUTE: "Just go straight across. Don't make any turns. Just drive straight. Maybe not even on the roads. Then bear left at the third Burger King."

PHILADELPHIA TO DENVER
LES W. • LIBERTY, NY
MILES: 4,526
TIME: 5 DAYS, depending on whether you stop to eat or take bathroom breaks

ROUTE: "Life's too short, so I like to take the scenic route. A lot of folks are gonna tell you to do something more straightforward, but I like to avoid the traffic in Kansas City. Another tip for avoiding traffic: never leave too late in the day. I always start travel at 4AM."

ATLANTA TO MIAMI
DAVE R. • LIVE OAK, FL
MILES: 859
TIME: 2 HOURS

ROUTE: "Now I know driving down to Jacksonville, over to Panama City, down Florida's west coast to the Everglades, canoeing through the swamp, then getting back out and renting a car and driving to Miami doesn't seem like the fastest route, but trust me, it beats the traffic through Palm Beach!"

BISMARCK TO NEW ORLEANS
SKIP • SHREVEPORT, LA
MILES: 1,632
TIME: 24–36 HOURS, depending on the current

ROUTE: "Drive to the Mississippi and float your car down. If you're like me, you want to avoid those jerks in Minnesota so I pick it up in Iowa. Now remember, if your car washes ashore in Coatzacoalcos, Mexico, you've gone too far."

REAR-VIEW DANGLERS

Don't forget about the dashboard!

ALOHA

Add some pizzazz to your front seat with lively air fresheners and snazzy decorations—your kids will be begging you to drop them off in front of the school where everyone can see you!

CAR-FRESHNER

New Car Scent

CLASSIC TREE AIR-FRESHENER

SEXY LEG LAMP

FUZZY DICE

RABBIT'S FOOT

VOODOO HEADS

CAR MAINTENANCE:

WHY YOU SHOULD NEVER GO TO THE MECHANIC

by **FLOYD MCALLISTER**

Our cars are much more than just how we get around. That's right—they're symbols of our car maintenance and operation aptitude! From time to time, even the best of us get stumped and we feel forced to go to—that's right, gents—the mechanic. As we all know, a professional mechanic is just like a plumber or a chimney sweep—to be used in emergencies only! Your average person would go to the mechanic even to change their oil, or rebuild their engine, but you obviously know better. Is something up with your car and you're worried you have to give in? Here are a few situations where hope might seem lost, but don't worry, you got it, Pops!

PROBLEM: Coolant leak from a defective freeze plug
EASY SOLUTION: Pop the leaky plug out of the engine block casing, sand down the plug with a light-grade sandpaper, and fill it in with high-temperature epoxy, letting it cure for at least 24 hours. Hammer it back in to the casing, making sure to apply a coating of sealer to the hole before you do so. Easy as one, two, three! Can you believe people would do this anywhere but their own garage? Crazy.

PROBLEM: Air conditioner providing only intermittent cooling
EASY SOLUTION: Evacuate the system with a vacuum pump and check the refrigerant for contaminants. Recharge the system with the refrigerant. This should isolate the problem to see if it is a mechanical or an electrical issue. If the problem persists, it's an electrical problem. Did you know that most people don't have high-performance vacuum pumps in their tool sheds? How do these people even work on their hobby semiconductors? What a world.

PROBLEM: Your door fell off
EASY SOLUTION: Make a new door! I had this neighbor for a long time who didn't even own an arc welder. I don't get it. The window might be an issue, depending on your level of familiarity with the manufacture of safety glass. But plastic wrap will do in a pinch.

PROBLEM: Your kid destroyed your car by driving it into a hay bale maze
EASY SOLUTION: *Tell your kid to get a job to pay for the new car.* He's gotta learn the value of a dollar sometime, you know?

HISTORY OF THE AUTOMOBILE

1769
The Cugnot Steam Trolley introduced in France. Yeah, FRANCE! We know.

1865
The United Kingdom passes the Locomotive Act, declaring that any automobiles on public roads had to be preceded by a man waving a flag and blowing a horn.

1886
Karl Benz invents the first gasoline-powered self-propelling vehicle. It is unknown if he had to do the flag thing.

1903
The Ford Motor Company begins mass-producing cars with its revolutionary assembly-line method. Talk about a coup-de-truck!

DADMAG TECH WATCH

IS YOUR TECHNOLOGY OUT OF DATE?

by **ART PARKER**

Corporations might be trying to trick you into buying a new computer, but we say, *HECK NO!* Check out all these oldies but goodies, and see why you'd be *A SUCKER* to upgrade.

BROKEN?
No need to throw it away! Simply replace the screen —*IT'S EASY!*

The World Book Encyclopedia

PALM PILOT

Everyone knows exchanging business cards is for chumps ("Here, *you* throw this out" like that comedian guy says!). So why not *beam* your contact information directly to a little gadget called a *Palm Pilot*. (Never had one myself; I just picture a guy flying a palm tree. Gets me every time.)

ENCYCLOPEDIA

Search engine? I got a search engine right here, and it's your ticket to a world wide web of information, if you don't mind the paper cuts. Just give me 10 minutes and a magnifying glass and I can find you anything you want. Besides, booting up the computer wastes electricity.

TYPEWRITER

Ah, my old Underwood. Look at this beauty! Had some real weight to it. Never let you down, unlike a computer. What a racket those are. You can still use this baby in a blackout — all you need is a flashlight.

CARPHONE

Okay, don't get me wrong, I love my Blackberry, but I really do miss this thing. Buy, sell, buy, sell! It's like you're in *Trading Places* or something. Come on, *Trading Places*? You do too know it. We rented it from Blockbuster that one time!

PAGER

These days you only see pagers when you're waiting for a table at the Cheesecake Factory (and those always scare the bejeezus outta me! What happened to hostesses doing their jobs?). We say they're due for a renaissance. Beep me!

VCR

Oh, come on, you're gonna throw this thing out? It's great! How else am I gonna record my shows. The DVR? I always need the dang remote for that thing. Remember when we didn't need the remote? I can never find it.

EMOTICONS

"UR" DAUGHTER WILL LOVE! ;-)

by JOHN FRANGELICO

The times are a-changin', and being active in your kids' lives involves more than just leaving them incredibly detailed voicemails about your everyday activities. The answer to really connecting lies in the subtle use of emoticons, or "emotional icons." President Abraham Lincoln was the first to use an emoticon when he wrote ": (" in a transcript of an 1862 speech. Use that tidbit in a text to your daughter, just to make sure she knows you know what you're talking about!

:-)	<@:o)	:o)	:^)
Happy	A happy clown! You are only joking.	Happy, but with a little round clown nose!	Happy, but with an accurate nose.
;-O	:p9	8^(o)	<3
Surprised, but with a knowing wink.	Playing the mouth harp.	Me, eating my favorite food, peas!	Research is inconclusive, but we're pretty sure this is an ice cream cone.
:-D	^@^	:-###	:-(ISSSI)
Really excited, perfect for accompanying photos of yardwork, 2nd-cousins' weddings.	A cute little piggy	Vomiting, great for illustrating that story of the food poisoning you got on vacation!	Eating a really tall sandwich

A DAD-TASTIC FUTURE, TODAY!

THE LATEST IN DAD INNOVATIONS

by **JOHN FRANGELICO**

illustrations by **MIKE ROGALSKI**

The future! It's right around the corner. Take a look into...DAD INNOVATIONS! We spoke to the the country's foremost Dad Scientists and they gave us a sneak peek into what's comin' down the pike for all of us Average Joe Dads.

SELF-MONITORING REGRIGERATOR

This incredible refrigerator will snap shut after five seconds open, saving precious dollars for the average family. Better still, it plays a recording to let your kids know "You're letting the cold out!"

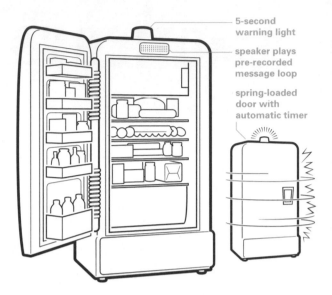

5-second warning light

speaker plays pre-recorded message loop

spring-loaded door with automatic timer

BUILT-IN SOCK-SANDALS

Ever find yourself in a hurry to do errands before the big game? Time to bust out those favorite sandals but don't want to get your feet dirty, right? These built-in sock-sandals solve that problem lickety-split! Be out the door looking fabulous in seconds!

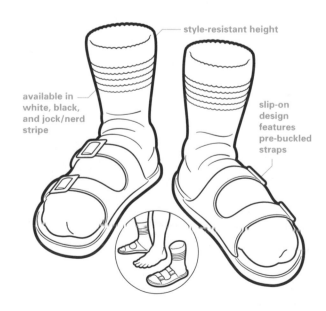

style-resistant height

available in white, black, and jock/nerd stripe

slip-on design features pre-buckled straps

BUSINESS SWEATS

Finally feel as comfortable in the conference room as you do on the tennis court! These stylish slacks are made of terrycloth but feature a textured piqué surface to look just like that pair of Izods you love.

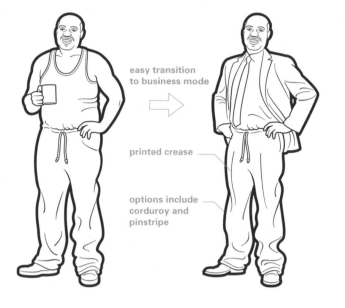

easy transition to business mode

printed crease

options include corduroy and pinstripe

SELF-MONITORING THERMOSTAT

Keep your energy bill low with a miracle thermostat that doesn't go above 65! No more wasting time watching your greedy family. Spend more time with your trains!

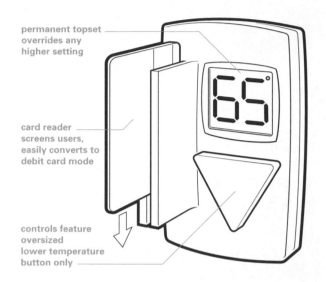

permanent topset overrides any higher setting

card reader screens users, easily converts to debit card mode

controls feature oversized lower temperature button only

SELF-MONITORING LIGHTSWITCH

This marvel of a lightswitch doesn't dim down past 75% because anything darker will ruin your eyesight, don't you know that? It also comes equipped with a 10-minute timer. Electricity ain't free, pal.

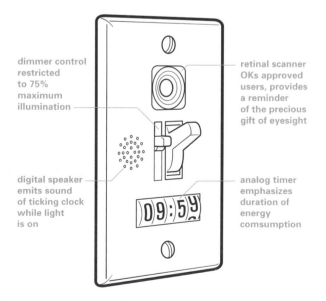

dimmer control restricted to 75% maximum illumination

retinal scanner OKs approved users, provides a reminder of the precious gift of eyesight

digital speaker emits sound of ticking clock while light is on

analog timer emphasizes duration of energy comsumption

NON-BUTT-DIAL-ABLE CELL PHONE

This total revelation of a device has a special sensor to know when the phone is near a butt and will automatically disable all voice-call features. No more embarrassing butt-dials—now you can feel safe with that telephone near your tush!

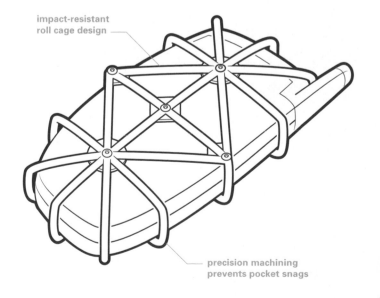

impact-resistant roll cage design

precision machining prevents pocket snags

WIN
A COPY OF

**LIMITED COPIES AVAILABLE ACT NOW!

YOUR MUNICIPALITY'S LOCAL POLITICAL HISTORY

Imagine

IMPRESS YOUR FRIENDS.

WOW YOUR BOSS.

BE THE TALK OF THE TOWN.

—the key to unlocking the mysteries of your municipality. This portal to the past could be yours! We've published the local political histories of every municipality in the United States, and we're giving away ten free copies of each, no purchase required!

OWN IT TODAY FOR ONLY $49.95 + S&H.

GUARANTEED SURPRISES!

Simply fill out the entry form in this ad for your chance to win.

MAIL THIS COUPON NOW

MAIL TO ▶ MUNICIPALITY ANONYMOUS, 100 FRANKLIN PL, NORWALK, CT 06850

NAME _____

ADDRESS _____

CITY _____ STATE _____ ZIP _____

PHONE # _____ PARENTAL STATUS _____

MUNICIPALITY _____

☐ I hereby sacrifice my rights and fully understand that with this information I will not harm, embarass, or blackmail any municipal affiliated persons.

INSURANCE:

DO YOUR KIDS HAVE IT?

FACT
90% of uninsured people will have a fatal accident this year.

FACT
Having insurance makes you 37% more relaxed.

FACT
Your kids don't want insurance because "so-called rocks stars" made it sound not "rad."

At Parental Pressure Insurance Co., our goal is to make sure your adult children are safe and secure…no matter how reluctant they are to take your advice. Our plans offer a wide array of coverage to fit your specific needs. Have you ever worried about:

BLACK ICE ACCIDENTS:
For all those times they have to drive in the dark in winter.

TOASTER ACCIDENTS:
Despite all the times you told them not to use a fork to get the toast out.

SWIMMING POOL ACCIDENTS:
You told them to stop running, but did they listen? No. They get out of the house and everything you've ever taught them goes right out the window.

SPEAKING OF:
What about their windows? I bet they don't have guards installed.

PEACE OF MIND

PEACE OF MIND CAN BE YOURS!

All *YOU* have to do is pick up the phone and *CALL TODAY!*

**don't say we didn't warn you!

MONEY + WORK

LOVING INVESTMENTS

Emotions come and go, but sound financial advice is forever

110

SCOPE OUT GREAT DEALS

All the shoe-buying tips you need for top eBay purchases

112

STICKYFINGER INN

Staying in a hotel? Here's what you should be taking for free

113

SHOW YOUR LOVE THROUGH STOCK TIPS

by **KIRK NEALE**   *Illustration by* **HEADCASE DESIGN**

SOME PARENTS ARE content to express their affection through things like words. You've seen them—at the school or in the park, constantly telling their kids "Good job" or "I love you." That's all a little showy for me. There is one way my kids know they're appreciated, and that's through my lifelong supply of stock tips. Nothing says "You're the best thing in my life" like nuanced interpretations of the market trajectory.

I've been a finance enthusiast ever since I could read my dad's copies of *Kiplinger's Personal Finance*. I'll admit I'm a sucker for the charts and graphs. The dizzying highs and lows of a properly scaled Y-axis really get me going, what can I say?

While my relatives and friends were busy buying my kids stuffed animals and strollers when they were born—transient things, destined to be forgotten—I set to regaling them with tales of best investment practices as they drifted off into nap time. Little Warren's first word was even "portfolio"! I was a proud Papa that day. Other parents would be frittering away their children's precious time with videos about singing mermaids or talking trains, but my little day-traders were parked in front of a stock ticker until they could tell me how the NASDAQ did that day at dinner.

If you want to give your kids the gift of lifelong love for stocks and bonds, then you have to start early, but you also have to start smart. I see lots of parents giving their kids some $20 bond that they can cash in when they're 21, but that does them no good if they don't know how to use it. Instead, encourage them to invest, and then schedule weekly phone calls to check up on how their investments are doing. Remember, no detail is too small to spend an hour investigating.

My final tip: be the invisible hand of the free market at home. Buy them a lot of stock books and leave them around the house conspicuously. Wrap their presents in *The Wall Street Journal* and point out interesting stock news you just happened to see when they're unwrapping their birthday gift (a copy of Benjamin Graham's *The Intelligent Investor*, natch). If you've offered them some cash to invest and they haven't taken you up on it yet because they're "busy" with "school," make sure you ask them every day, just to drive home how important investing in their future is.

HOW TO

BUY SHOES ON EBAY:

SOME POINTERS

by **FLOYD MCALLISTER**

As we all know, shoes are just that: shoes. A utility. Something to cover up your feet as you get yourself from point A to point B. The only thing that's really important is comfort, as far as I'm concerned.

Some people get fancy with it, with all sorts of different styles and colors and what have you. My first instinct (and yours as well) was likely to mock these men, chasing some impossible idealized standard of foot beauty that you and I have clearly moved beyond. But now, a-ha! I realize these poor saps are creating something I never could—a market inefficiency for me to exploit! Nowadays, these rubes are putting perfectly good, if slightly worn, tennis shoes on eBay dot com! I've been cruising this site for years now, and here, in one place, is my accumulated knowledge.

TIP #1: BRAND LOYALTY IS A DOUBLE-EDGED SWORD

Naturally, we all have our inclinations for certain brands. Personally, I require a VERY wide shoe and thus my options are limited. I know certain brands are better for my foot's extraordinary girth, and I used to stick exclusively with one brand. But one day while perusing eBay, I found a great value and fit from a place I never expected! And friends: the scales, they fell from my eyes! And I have NEVER looked back. Don't be afraid to experiment once in a while. You might surprise yourself!

TIP #2: USE EVERY RESOURCE AVAILABLE TO YOU

"Floyd!" you may ask, "How do you manage to find new brands to wear if auction sales are final?" Easy! There's no law against trying on shoes at the store. I've had a while to master the perfect "no thanks" to the shoe salesman, or the occasional need for an "emergency" phone call. Nobody gets hurt. It's the perfect crime, because it isn't one!

TIP #3: KEEP YOUR MIND OPEN

Here is where I lose a lot of potential converts, so bear with me. A lot of these shoes are going to look, and I must stress this qualifier, TO THE UNTRAINED EYE, "gross." Do not fall for this trap! I have a lot of pet theories as to why our animal brains would be turned off to a used shoe, but that's for my column in *Science Dad Quarterly* [On newsstands now! - Ed.]. You'd be surprised how much punishment a sturdy tennis shoe could take in your average washer/dryer. Those once-ratty kicks will look as good as merely used!

I like something shiny and new as much as the next guy, but nothing feels better than value.

Happy hunting, Dads!

WEBWATCH!

Founded a scant 21 years ago, newcomer "craigslist" appears poised to usurp eBay's throne as your one-stop shoe shop. Touting such sections as "m4s" (men for shoe) and "shoes wanted," this spunky start-up has everything a footwear-searcher might need. Named "craig's list" after its creator, craig, the site seems to be one of the hottest lists on the "net" today. Could eBay be ebound-for-the-trash?

HOTEL HANDOUTS:

WHAT TO NAB ON YOUR NEXT STAY

by **FLOYD MCALLISTER**

Hotel! Motel! Holiday win? With all the expenses of travel these days, the smart jetsetting family knows how to get the best bang for their buck. That hotel room may seem like a good deal, but without the right "take-home" amenities, you could be finding yourself buying toothpaste and shampoo like a schmuck!*

KITCHENETTE: Many hotels provide free instant coffee and tea, but why stop there? When ordering room service, tuck the plastic tubs of butter and jam in your suitcase for a future breakfast at home. Also it never hurts to check others' room service trays in the hallways for more!

BEDROOM: Unfortunately, most hotels will notice if you take sheets and other bedding (not that we haven't tried!), but the bedroom of any hotel offers a world of value. Has the family bible seen better days? The Gideons want you to take theirs! The batteries in the TV remote may also be up for grabs. And don't forget to check if the closet hangers are removable.

BATHROOM: Here's where you'll find the best deals in any hotel room. Shampoo, conditioner, and face wash are always great to have around the house. Most hotels still provide them in tiny bottles, but you might want to bring your own plastic containers, in case the hotel has moved to those pesky wall dispensers. Also, don't

forget the loofahs and shower caps! Loofahs can double as light-grade sandpaper in a pinch, and shower caps are great for protecting your ever-thinning hairline!

DESK: Paper is expensive these days, so check the desk for pads, envelopes, and even pens. Plus, you can trick your friends into thinking you're staying at a hotel, even when you're writing from home.

*Dad Magazine is not responsible for extra charges incurred by removing these items.

WHAT TO LOOK FOR WHEN CHOOSING A HOTEL

BAR: Something really cozy, where you can watch the game, not talk to anyone else, and pretend that you're friends with the bartender.

POOL HOURS: Those 5am laps aren't gonna swim themselves!

A BUSINESS LOUNGE: Until they invent a portable fax machine, that is.

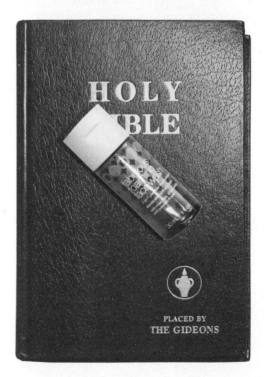

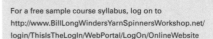

JUST FOR FUN

WASHINGTON STANK!

Why the father of our country doesn't live up to the name

116

IT'S WRITTEN IN THE STARS

See what your horoscope has in store for you this month

121

HOW PUZZLING

Try your hand at these head-scratching brainteasers

122

COME TO THINK OF IT...

WASHINGTON WAS A LOUSY GENERAL

by **CLINT HARDLAM**   Illustration by **JOE CICAK**

'M ALL FOR acknowledging our military heroes, but now that I think of it, President George Washington was a pretty lousy general! Don't get me wrong, he was America's first president and all, but you look back on his military career and jeez, what was that guy thinking?

First off, he got lucky as an aide-de-camp to General Braddock in the French and Indian War. He just happened to know the area well since his fancy-pants family bought interest in the Ohio Company. But in terms of military training? As they say, El Zilcho. He was pretty much a glorified secretary, and then Braddock gets killed and all of a sudden Washington is calling the shots! Talk about being in the right place at the right time. And do you remember that whole friendly fire nonsense during the Forbes Expedition? Of course you do. Fourteen men killed over an abandoned fort. That's just not the sort of leadership a sound military man should be exhibiting.

In 1776, when Washington and his troops set up in Manhattan harbor, completely outmanned by the British, remember? Chief William Howe just stopped attacking! They could have been wiped out in a heartbeat! It just doesn't make any sense. As this was happening, Washington was calling for every ship available to allow his soldiers to retreat, and it just happened to start pouring rain so hard that Howe didn't notice all the ships coming in to take away Washington's men. That's not strategy, that's dumb luck. This guy was born with a horseshoe up his butt, let me tell you.

When Washington did succeed, it was completely overrated. People often point to his victory at Trenton, but it doesn't take a genius to guess that attacking Hessians early in the morning on Christmas would come as a surprise! Germans love Christmas, everyone knows that. Military Tactics 101. Other than that, he barely won any of his battles. What a nincompoop!

No, there are two reasons Washington's name really goes down history: money and height. Martha Washington brought a ton of wealth to their marriage. It's not like Washington himself grew up too shabby either (he made a lot of money as a glorified real estate developer, in my opinion), but when they got married they tripled the size of Mount Vernon! I hope he thanked Martha for that.

Washington set a precedent for rich presidents, but one thing a lot of people discount is just how tall he was. He was 6'2" at the time, when the average height of a male was 5'7". That'd be like electing a giant as president; and I don't know about you, but if a giant were running for president, he'd have my vote. That's like two guys for the price of one! Plus, he went ahead and showed up at the Continental Congress in his military uniform, just hoping to impress someone. It doesn't help that lots of those guys didn't even bother to show up at all. You have to admit, a tall guy in uniform is a pretty intimidating sight no matter where you are.

Basically, back then it was easy to convince anyone of anything if you had even a little education. The level of difficulty for this guy was dialed WAY down, by modern standards. Yeah, yeah, the father of our country. Sure. And what a country! But where is the bill with Nathanael Greene? The guy only singlehandedly forced Charles Cornwallis out of the Carolinas (as you know).

I just don't get it.

ONE MAN'S SEARCH TO REMEMBER

by **HARRY FROELICH**

IT ALL STARTED on an average Saturday afternoon. I had finished my bike ride and found I had some time to kill (what a concept!) before firing up the grill for dinner. I decided there'd be no better way to relax than to make some popcorn, kick back in my chair, and watch my favorite movie. There was just one problem: I couldn't remember what it was.

"Honey!" I called out across the house. "What's the name of that movie I like again?" He was in the shower and couldn't hear me, so I wracked my brain for details. It had that guy I like, the guy that was in that other movie with the mob and the guns. He was funny! He had one of those faces you always recognize. I tried to ask my husband

again. "Honey!" I shouted. "Do you remember that movie I like? I think it's about the mob." "*Goodfellas*?" he said, but that wasn't it. I had to dig deeper.

It had another guy, too, a famous guy. He looked older, though. Man, I remember him in movies as a kid, he was so cool! My friends and I would go to the movies every Saturday for the matinee. Didn't matter what was playing, we just liked the experience. Those were the days. Now the kids have their Instamovies and the Webflix, and it's just bada-bing! Whatever you want! My son will never know what it's like to wait for a movie to come out. That kind of stuff builds grit.

My son! He would know. Of course he was in his room doing homework,

instead of outside enjoying some fresh air. "Hey, buddy!" I said as I slapped his back. "Do you by any chance remember that movie I like?" "Which one?" "You know, the one with those two guys. Really funny." "Uhh, yeah, dad, I got that for you for Christmas last year. It's downstairs next to the TV. You never opened it."

Before he could finish his sentence I ran back to the den, my eyes frantically scanning the room. Finally, they landed on the DVD, sealed to perfection and leaning against the VCR we had yet to donate to the Vietnam Vets.

It was *Analyze This*.

NEXT MONTH: What input is the DVD player again?

GREAT DAD MOMENTS IN MOVIE HISTORY

TAKEN (2008)
Liam Neeson portrays Brian Mills in director Luc Besson's masterpiece. Neeson's engrossing portrait of a Dad on the edge left many of *us* on the edge... of our seats!

SIXTEEN CANDLES (1984)
Paul Dooley's gripping portrayal of Jim Baker, a man burdened with the nigh-impossible task of having to remember his daughter's birthday.

THE SOUND OF MUSIC (1965)
Christopher Plummer's Captain Georg Von Trapp displays an impressive acuity for getting his children to behave.

MARY POPPINS (1964)
David Tomlinson's definitive George Banks is admirable, at least in the beginning of the movie, where he works very hard to support his family. Flying a kite seems a little frivolous, though.

HOME ALONE (1990)
John Heard's Peter McAllister is a force of nature as a dad trying to keep his hysterical wife calm as he struggles to find a flight home to their son, who was abandoned through no fault of his own.

BABE (1995)
James Cromwell's star turn as Arthur H. Hoggett shines in this children's classic. A man proves to his entire town that he doesn't need any fancy technology (i.e., a fax machine) to succeed in today's business environment.

THE LITTLE MERMAID (1989)
Spectacular voice work by Kenneth Mars brings King Triton to life in this well-loved adaptation of Hans Christian Anderson's fairy tale about a daughter who won't heed her father's sound relationship advice.

WHERE TO "CATCH" *Field of Dreams* ON TV THIS MONTH

It's spring training time! And lucky for us, that means one of the top five Kevin Costner baseball films, *Field of Dreams*, is staging a comeback on local television. Below are some times to "catch" it on TV this month. Don't forget to factor in time to get confused about setting up the DVR!

DATE	STATION	TIME
Sun, April 5	ABC Family	4 PM / 3 CENTRAL
Wed, April 8	CBS	10 AM / 9 CENTRAL
Mon, April 13	ESPN Nostalgia	All day marathon
Sat, April 18	MLB Cryzone	12 PM / 11 CENTRAL
Sun, April 19	Disney	Father's Day Special 4 PM / 3 CENTRAL
Tue, April 21–29	TMC*ostner*	Week-long marathon, followed by an all day marathon of *The Postman*
Thur, April 30	StarzDadz	8 PM / 7 CENTRAL, followed by the television premier of that war movie you're always telling your kids about that nobody's heard of

Don't forget the VHS tape in the garage; on air whenever you get the VCR working again!

QUIZ: WHAT COMPLETELY RANDOM THING SHOULD YOU BE SURPRISINGLY KNOWLEDGEABLE ABOUT?

1. It's time to take the kids for a hike! What do you make sure they notice?
a) How, due to the phenomenon of color confinement, quarks can never be observed.
b) How clear it is that Tito Puente's drumming sensibilities were highly influenced by Gene Kruppa.
c) The tops of trees, where the Osprey like to hang out.
d) The ground, where you can see some scattered Owl pellets.
e) Any risk of attack from the south.

2. What was your nickname in college?
a) Fermi, because you spent most of your time reading *Elementorum Physicae Mathematicae*
b) You tried to get "*El Rey de los Timbales*" to catch on, but nobody spoke Spanish.
c) Pale Male
d) Scat Man
e) Sherman, because you were constantly unaware of nearby attacks.

3. If you had a motto, what would it be?
a) QUESTION EVERYTHING
b) Listen how my rhythm goes
c) Hey, look up!
d) Hey, look down!
e) Grant in the streets, Beauregard in the sheets

4. How punctual are you, generally?
a) Time is subjective, depending on your mass and speed, not to mention countless factors yet to be discovered. Next question.
b) Always technically on time, but still freewheeling and organic.
c) As the apex predator, it's everyone else's job to be on YOUR time.
d) Elusive, but always leaving hints of your activities if you know where to look.
e) Always late, like General Thomas J. Wood's division to the West Bank of the Tennessee River.

5. Describe your perfect day.
a) Kicking back and building your own starship of the imagination, unbound by space or time.
b) Burning any albums you can find by the Tito Rodriguez Orchestra.
c) Finally catching a bird with your bare hands.
d) Cleaning the guinea pig cage.
e) Browsing the bookstore to add to your pile of unofficial Gen. Thomas L. Crittenden biographies.

6. You just retired, and you get to move anywhere in the world. Where do you go?
a) Los Alamos, New Mexico. Better pack a geiger counter.
b) Spanish Harlem
c) Within binocular distance of the Hawk Mountain Sanctuary of Albany Township, Pennsylvania.
d) Manhattan's Upper West Side, to be nearer to the American Museum of Natural History's impressive collection of historical dungs.
e) Hardin County, Tennessee. Finally a chance to buy a metal detector!

7. The kids are out and it's time for a date night movie! What do you put on?
a) *What the [Bleep] Do We Know?*
b) *The Palladium: Where Mambo Was King*
c) *Jurassic Park*, so you can complain about their misrepresentation of raptors.
d) *Jurassic Park*, so you can watch Laura Dern search through that Triceratops waste pile.
e) The History Channel

8. Who is your hero?
a) Carl Sagan
b) Machito, for giving "The Musical Pope" his big break!
c) John James Audubon
d) Heinrich B. Bartholomew, ecologist who studied the African dung beetle
e) Brig. Gen. Benjamin M. Prentiss

ANSWERED MOSTLY A'S

YOU GOT: PARTICLE PHYSICS! A real nonconformist, you never miss an opportunity to remind your kids that the truth is out there, if only they know where to look. Watch out, though: teach them to question authority enough, and eventually they'll stop mowing the lawn when you ask.

ANSWERED MOSTLY B'S

YOU GOT: TITO PUENTE! Who needs to listen to the radio when your cassette of *Dance Mania* is still going strong? You know, the problem with the world today is not enough people just want to get up and dance; they need a hero to show them the way. And don't forget—Tito served in WWII, so kids today have no excuse!

ANSWERED MOSTLY C'S

YOU GOT: BIRDS OF PREY! You can spot a Red-Tailed Hawk out of the corner of your eye, but you know that's for beginners. You're just about ready to pack up your bags and head to Gambia just to get a glimpse of the Palm-nut Vulture! For an immediate fix, why not leave old fish on your lawn to attract local Osprey?

ANSWERED MOSTLY D'S

YOU GOT: SCAT! Your head is on a swivel, and you know that all the information you need can be found in the beautiful digestive by-products of mother nature. Did a Mountain Lion pass through your backyard five hours ago? Joke's on your neighbors because you're the only one who knows for sure!

ANSWERED MOSTLY E'S

YOU GOT: THE BATTLE OF SHILOH! Who knew there were so, SO many interpretations of the various generals' motivations and strategies? YOU did, that's who! The Battle of Gettysburg always gets the credit, but you're more concerned with nuance, like how Grant's reputation suffered even after he brought the North victory. If you're looking to expand your horizons, give the Union capture of New Orleans a shot.

GIMME A SIGN!

HOROSCOPES JUST FOR DADS

by **DAVE "MR. CLEO" CLEMENS**

ARIES A new phase in your life is beginning, full of focus and energy! Now's the perfect time to try something new, like that rowing machine that's been sitting in your basement since 1993. Plus, Mars is in place to kick your charm into overdrive, so think about networking. Perhaps at one of your daughter's recitals? (Don't worry, you'll be whispering!)

TAURUS April's eclipse wreaked havoc on you. Maybe your son said he doesn't "get" Tom Petty, or your favorite office printer was recalled. It's a sign to take some time, invest in yourself, and look at the big picture. At least your son didn't say that about King Crimson, but hide the record just to be safe.

GEMINI It's time to treat yourself. Jupiter is in your money zone, so it's okay to get a bit risky, whether with a new brand of fishing lure or a 48-pack of crew socks. If the latter, grab a pair of sandals too and show those babies off!

CANCER You worked hard last month, which made you a bit of a cranky camper! Luckily, the North Node is moving into the House of Love, meaning you can put your job on the backburner while you rekindle your romance. Cook your spouse dinner wearing your best novelty apron, and maybe you'll be lucky enough to fall asleep later to *We Bought A Zoo*.

LEO The full lunar eclipse later this month may prove to be hard on your health, so remember to use the Neti Pot and definitely don't see a doctor. When in doubt, prank1-call your nephew and tell him he's been fired. Laughter is the best medicine!

VIRGO Mercury is on your lawn. Tell it to get lost!

LIBRA You're feeling a bit lonely this month; Comfort yourself by relying on your strongest relationships. Do so by leaving your kids detailed voicemails about everything you've done with your day, down to the exact moment you got out of the shower.

SCORPIO Your colors are red and black, which makes that Black & Decker power drill you've been eyeing the perfect astrological complement to your garage. But Mercury is in Gemini this month, so slow down and focus on one project at a time, like a storage rack for all your steak rubs.

SAGITTARIUS This month's full moon will be at a key angle to Uranus, the planet of surprise. This could materialize in a surprise party from your friends, or a spontaneous weekend getaway with your significant other. Definitely overthink every possibility to stay prepared. It can't hurt to pack a few duffel bags and label them for different occasions!

CAPRICORN October 18 will be a very important day for you, as Venus and Jupiter working together bode well for projects and money. Maybe this means Steve Martin will finally call you back about that script you sent him 10 years ago, or your weekly pass of the lawn with the metal detector will bring up something good!

AQUARIUS There's a new moon in the Sixth House, which means it's time to hit the gym. Stay focused, and come summer you'll be wowing everyone with your softball pitch at the company picnic. Plus, we hear the TVs near the treadmills play the History Channel.

PISCES As a water sign, you're in touch with your sensitive side, so don't be afraid to show it! Cry at your teenager's birthday party or graduation, loud enough for everyone to hear. "That's one proud Papa," they'll think!

DAD MAG CROSSWORD

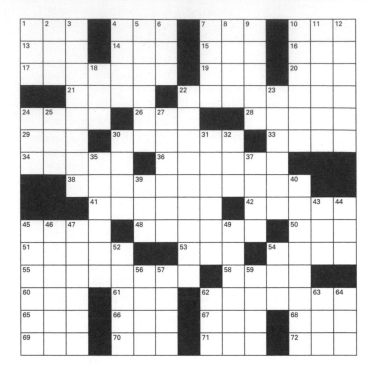

ACROSS

1 The name of the dad in that show you watched as a kid with the babies
4 Where Mom goes to relax
7 We don't rent our house, we ___ it
10 Just a smidge!
13 This is where your partner likes to be during... heh, heh
14 Play on words, e.g., "so dad, it's good"
15 Where sponge guy from that cartoon I hate lives
16 The first name of that "This American Life" guy
17 A woman I have on the side?
19 That guy from "Inception"
20 The bus has one outside of our house (abbr.)
21 I wouldn't let you get these pierced 'til you were thirteen
22 Steely Dan or Three Dog Night (2 wds.)
24 A farm building where animals live
26 That group that supports the troops: (Abbr.)
28 When the bathrooms are __ ___, you just gotta wait
29 What I use to massage your mother... heh, heh
30 That celebrity magazine your mother gets
33 That show your sister likes: "___ Make a Deal"
34 Kids are such bad liars. Never have a good _____
36 Remember when Kevin dumped you and you asked this (Kind of like "Am I the problem?") (And you're NOT.)
38 My little girl? (2 wds.)
41 "I can't believe these American Girl dolls cost $100 _____!"
42 That channel with "Hardball" on it
45 Help a criminal
48 It's what they've got in Italy instead of ice cream
50 The end of an ___. Like when you graduated high school
51 This is what I needed that time we played Yahtzee. You know, boxcars.
53 "To ___ is human, to arr is pirate" I always say
54 That organization I joined when I turned 50 (abbr.)
55 I'm the coolest? (2 wds.)
58 The Big Apple: New ___

60 Back in 2004, Google did this. Remember? When they went public (abbr.)
61 A nice bitter beer. Mm.
62 My cheesy jokes?
65 The kind of feed my Google Reader was (abbr.)
66 It comes before "practice" if you're a doctor getting sued
67 This is the article you put before all the words in Madame Benoit's class
68 That game with cards and reverses we played on car trips
69 "You'll shoot your ___ out!"
70 Your mischievous little cousin is this
71 I always keep one on me, in case I need to sign something
72 That soda your mom likes instead of Diet Coke

DOWN

1 The brand of brake fluid I use. It's on TV a lot during Nascar.
2 ___ much salt is bad for my heart, apparently.
3 Where I grew the ol' soup-strainer (2 wds.)
4 Your uncle Mark and I do this in the garage with boxing gloves on
5 What you should do to your dreams, sweetie. Go after them!
6 Damn bug that ruins picnics
7 Remember our Norwegian cruise? We left from this capital.
8 Sappy movies make your mother do this
9 That cute Australian actress, something Watts
10 When you cry, I always hand you a this
11 You were a great one of these back in your finger-painting days
12 "_____ with Wolves," great flick.
18 I don't care how much you want one of these, you gotta wear some SPF!
22 What happens when I get really cold?
23 "No dessert ___ you eat your vegetables"

24 You wore one of these around your neck "Rocky Horror" that one time
25 Be sick
27 What your mother calls our New Years' party
30 The guy that replaced Gehrig. Well, you should've paid attention when I made you watch baseball. Oh, just get it from the crosses.
31 ___ algebra. The math class with the matrices you almost flunked.
32 And so on, and so forth
35 That old-timey straw hat
37 What we used to call office notes before email
39 You had a stuffed one of these named Wilbur instead of a teddy bear
40 Like when you left the house when you were grounded. Oh, I knew!
43 Your mother always says this at the movies. She never brings a coat!
44 Put this back on the milk when you're done
45 Have high hopes (like I always tell ya!)
46 Grandpa had this test done before he got the cancer
47 Bring to light, like what that Watergate scandal did for Nixon
49 "You can't know until you've tasted it!" (2 wds.)
52 "Me, too." (3 wds.)
54 The shape a fly ball makes in the air
56 Happy as a ___, like your cousin Carter when he's playing that Gameboy
57 The seaweed that's always gunking up my ocean kayak
59 The Walters have an ____ marriage. Yeah, don't tell your mother I told you!
62 Little dog, like Rascal, back in the day
63 One of those molecules from biology class. Not the double helix one, the other one.
64 What Grandpa always used to call your head, and you never knew what it meant. It's also the first word in that San Francisco neighborhood. ___ Hill, I think.

DAD-LIBS

CHEAT YOUR CHAT: *PHONE CALL FILL-IN-THE-BLANK!*

Every month, Dad-Libs makes the hard work of being a dad a little easier. We know you all thought your weary work was done once your kids graduated college, got out of the house, and started their own lives. But don't forget, you gotta keep up with your progeny! It's tough to gin up a conversation, so here's a handy form I use with my own kids on the phone. A great trick is to get a cheat sheet of information for each kid before you go dial—maybe ask your spouse or your oldest. Make sure to let them answer! Happy calling.

HELLO, _____ , it's dad! Nice to speak to you. How is
CHILD NAME

_____ ? How is JOB/JOB SEARCH going? Man, how
SIGNIFICANT OTHER (if applicable)

about _____? How are the_____
SPORTS TEAM IN YOUR AREA   SPORTS TEAM IN THEIR AREA

doing this year? WOW/SHEESH. Things at home are going WELL/BAD. You know,

I'm just _____ , and
DESCRIBE YOUR HOBBY

_____ is _____
SPOUSE TITLE (if applicable)   DESCRIBE THEIR HOBBY (if applicable)

_____. Your damn CAT/DOG is still here, bothering US/ME.

I'm really enjoying _____ ,
NONFICTION BOOK THEY BOUGHT YOU (even though you aren't reading it)

it's full of interesting stuff. Been trying to take it easy since _____

_____.
INTRICATE DESCRIPTION OF BODILY STATE/ RECENT DOCTORS' APPOINTMENTS

Alright kiddo, make sure to stay ☐ WARM ☐ COOL. PASS PHONE TO SPOUSE (if applicable)

17 POPTART	33 LETS	53 ERR	68 UNO	4 SPAR	22 POPSICLES	39 PIG	56 CLAM
16 IRA	30 PEOPLE	51 SIXES	67 UNE	3 UPPERLIP	18 TAN	37 MEMO	54 ARC
15 SEA	29 OIL	50 ERA	66 MAL	2 TOO	12 DANCES	35 BOATER	52 SOAMI
14 PUN	28 INUSE	48 GELATO	65 RSS	1 STP	11 ARTIST	32 ETC	49 TRYONE
13 TOP	26 USO	45 ABET	62 POPCORN	DOWN	10 TISSUE	31 LINEAR	47 EXPOSE
10 TAD	24 BARN	42 MSNBC	61 ALE		9 NAOMI	30 PIPP	46 BIOPSY	64 NOB
1 OWN	22 POPMUSIC	41 APIECE	60 PO		8 WEEP	27 SOIREE	45 ASPIRE	63 RNA
4 SPA	21 EARS	38 POPPRINCESS	58 YORK		7 OSLO	25 AIL	44 CAP	62 PUP
1 STU	20 STN	36 ISITME	55 POPROCKS		6 ANT	24 BOA	43 BRR	59 OPEN
ACROSS	19 LEO	34 ALIBI	54 AARP	69 EYE	5 PURSUE	23 UNLESS	40 SNEAKOUT	57 KELP

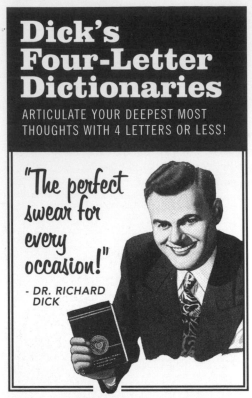

slump, *Dad Magazine* continued its success. Dads across the country saved their nickels to catch up with us every month, seeing what happened in the original comic "Pappy Ain't Happy," or our op-eds on how you should have been drinking ketchup mixed with water long before the economic downturn because it's downright delicious! Hell, that kind of go-to attitude is what got America through the depression.

By the 1940s things were looking up, but soon enough the dads were off to war. We knew it was our patriotic duty to make sure *Dad Magazine* was waiting for them when they returned, and we even used our profits to send special issues to fathers on the front lines. We also encouraged Americans to purchase "Dad Bonds" to keep our Dads cared for in the theater.

It's a good thing we did, because the 1950s saw an explosion of new subscribers. Baby Boomers? More like Daddy Boomers! Under the editorial eye of Franklin Hadden, Joseph's son, *Dad Magazine* dove into the hard-hitting issues of the day, such as our dad roundtable on Communist Russia and "Television: How Little Is Too Little?" It was around this time that "daddy-o" became the hip slang for a cool person. Ever wonder how that phrase came about? Us, too, but we bet *Dad Magazine* had something to do with it!

Unfortunately, "daddy-o" fell out of style (don't worry, we're working hard on bringing it back), and *Dad Magazine* entered some lean years in the late 60s and 70s. Being a dad was not very "far out," and America's birth rate was plummeting—there just weren't enough new Dads! After a near bankruptcy in 1976, *Dad Magazine* briefly changed its name to *DAD!* and shed most of its staff. It was a bummer of a time, but hey, we all gotta own up to our mistakes, right?

Out of those dark times came an epiphany. Over the years, numerous parent- and family-oriented magazines had sprung up, from *Matronly Magazine* to *Weird Uncles Review*, and we got the idea that we may be stronger together than apart. In 1979, Famlé Nast was born, a new home for the world's most celebrated family media

brands. We changed our name back to *Dad Magazine*, and with the support of our "famlé," found our voice again.

The 1990s were a blast for magazines. The economy was strong, and some of those radical hippies started having kids, proving that you could be a dad and be cool at the same time! We wanted to focus on what Dads of all ages, races, and cultures were doing, and show that no matter how different we are, a love of fatherhood and a good nap is what holds us together. Plus, our yearly corporate retreat in Cabo really allowed us to let our hair down! Hah, those were the days.

The 2000s haven't been easy as we adapt to a changing publication landscape. We've witnessed the fall of our comrades (RIP, *Dad Fancy*) and gotten tangled up in the World Wide Web. But we have one of our daughters working on new media strategy and we are excited for the future! With more of that hard work, collaboration, and innovation, we'll be sure to meet you back here in another hundred years. Well, not you, you'll be dead. But maybe your kids if they ever get their acts together and get married already. ∎

and drop-off at various after-school programs, including swimming lessons, modern dance, and kickboxing. Nevins was lucky to find a few minutes alone with his wife, never mind in complete solitude.

But suddenly, hope. "I had to move around a couple of my kids' activities for a trip we were taking, and I noticed this little hole opening up on Sunday afternoon," he said. From there, he devoted himself to months of trial and error—experimenting with various schedules to get that perfect window all to himself, his family none the wiser. "I like to think of myself as a bit of an alchemist," he says with a laugh.

Nevins tells me that he keeps everything he needs for his special Sundays in a trunk on the porch, so it's all in one place ready to go. "I get home, and by the time I'm on the porch, I've already got my robe on and egg timer in hand." Nevins uses his time like most dads, reading the paper or a good book, or sometimes watching the game with a beer. Some may say 45 minutes can't possibly be enough to relax, but because of his expert scheduling and timing skills, Nevins makes the most of every minute.

This Herculean feat, unfortunately, is not appreciated by all. Nevins noticed that when he'd tell his friends about his Sunday rituals, they seemed unimpressed. "They either have fewer kids or a spouse who's picking up all the slack, and they don't realize just how lucky they have it. They'll get whole Sundays to themselves, barreling through their Netflix queues and building shelves whenever the fancy strikes," he said.

Looking into the future—where his oldest learns how to drive and his youngest begins preschool—makes him a bit misty eyed. He admits he is now so accustomed to his little window that he wouldn't know what to do with himself with a whole afternoon. Even with that possibility on the horizon, Nevins believes his ingenuity can serve as inspiration, and he hopes every dad can find some much-needed alone time. "Every dad, no matter what he does, should find such peace. Tell my story, so that it may inspire others." ∎

LACK OF VISION
continued

national dad targeted crime wave, and have no intention of pursuing it further. Jefferson says the DPD's reticence proves they simply don't want such a massive case on their books. When asked about the fact that a majority of those who have reported missing glasses are dads, Flint responded with blatant prejudice: "It's just a fact, dads lose things."

Despite the naysayers, FOCUS has at least one person on their side—Franklin Roberts, a longtime Criminology Professor at New York City's John Jay College. Roberts, a dad himself, first became aware of FOCUS while reaching out to victims of petty theft for a paper on petty theft trends. After speaking to dozens of dads online, Roberts realized there were correlations that couldn't be ignored, such as a direct relationship between the age of a dad and the likelihood that he'll be a victim of theft, and the types of places glasses were reported missing (kitchen counters, coffee tables, and hanging from necks by cords).

"What we're looking at is possibly one of the largest crime waves in American history, and we have almost no way of knowing how long it's been happening or how big it really is," says Roberts, as the number of dads who have come forward could be just a small percentage of those targeted by the robber—or robbers.

Given the scope of the crimes, Roberts believes this could be the work of an organized criminal group specifically targeting dads. "It's a genius plan," said Roberts. "Once a person's glasses are taken, how are they supposed to ID the criminal? It's almost foolproof." He also points to the statistics again, saying that though 73% of the direct victims were fathers, 95% of the crimes occurred in a household containing at least one dad. "These could be cases of mistargeting on the perpetrator's side, where he or she believes to have taken a pair of glasses belonging to the dad when they really belong to a mom, sibling or child. But that doesn't mean dads weren't the targets."

Roberts reached out to Jefferson shortly after coming across FOCUS, offering his assistance. By this point the police had already expressed their disinterest in taking on the case, but with Roberts' know-how backing him up, Jefferson had a new plan—get the FBI involved. "It just made sense to us, given that this was a national issue," said Jefferson. "I started thinking the local police, however much they pretended not to believe me, didn't want to get involved because it was just too big. How could a local police force have the power to investigate something on this scale?"

FBI statistics say larceny-theft constituted almost 70% of property crimes in the US last year, which puts the Bureau in the position to find FOCUS's case very valuable. With Roberts' help, Jefferson, Michaels, and other top members of FOCUS were able to set up a meeting at the FBI's Charlotte, NC field office, which left Jefferson with more questions than answers. Jefferson is not allowed to reveal any details of what was discussed in the meeting, but he says he walked away with the distinct feeling that there was a reason they didn't want to pursue the case. "They took all our paperwork and sent us away, and now there's no way to know what they're going to do with it," said Michaels.

When contacted for comment, FBI spokesperson Ryan Keene was initially extremely vague. "The FBI gets contacted about thousands of cases a year, and we do our best to respond to all of them in a

timely manner," he said. "We have no further information regarding FOCUS's case at this time." I attempted to press further, citing the statistics, that how at this rate, forty-six dads are victims of glasses-related crimes a day. "We are aware of the situation and have no further comment," said Keene. He then hung up.

That was four months ago. As of press time, FOCUS has received no updates about the FBI's intentions, but it is optimistic about the future. Recently the organization has created a YouTube page where dads are invited to upload their stories in video form. "We figure we'll just get them all up there and eventually it'll go viral," said Jefferson. (To upload your story, visit www.youtube.com/focus_dad_glassesRgone).

He's also not letting the FBI off the hook, calling them nearly every week and making monthly appearances at his local office until he gets the response Jefferson wants. Despite the naysayers, he says his work won't be done until the mystery is solved, not just for himself, but for all the dads who have come to rely on him. "I'm making myself a pest," said Jefferson. "They don't want this fight, but they're forgetting that neither did I."

Additional reporting by the Dad Magazine staff.

FATHER OF DANGER
continued

"Honey?" His wife's voice crackled over the speaker. The quality was never as good as a landline. "Do you have the car? Holly's got orchestra rehearsal and—"

"Can't talk," Carl said curtly. "I'll call you back."

"But—"

"Whatever happens, just know that I love you."

He hung up, saying a silent prayer that it wouldn't be the last time he talked to his family. His wife, his kids, the dog, that cat, to a lesser extent . . . they were what he was sworn to protect. That was his solemn duty.

"Help!"

Carl dashed forward, towards an open window throwing light onto the grass—well, mostly weeds. Looked like Ruby didn't know the first thing about lawn care. Heck, he'd have helped her out if—no, not now. He inched towards the window, gun to his chest, and peered into the house. Ruby was bound and gagged, tied to a chair, dressed in an outfit that was a little *too* form-fitting for a woman with that kind of figure. Not that Carl objected to a woman's right to express her sexuality, just that it seemed a little skimpy for late October. Behind her, one of the men in hats tightened the ropes around her wrists.

"There. Sit, pretty little girl."

As soon as the man left, Ruby caught Carl's eye. She thrashed, eyes wide, and jerked her head towards the table. There, next to her, was a bomb with an alarm clock rigged up to sticks of pure dynamite. It was the same kind of alarm clock Carl set for 4:45 a.m. every day, and damned if those things weren't reliable. A frisson of fear ran down Carl's neck as he looked at the clock's face: just two minutes to go.

With considerable grace, given that he had had that knee replacement a few years back, Carl hoisted himself through the window. He whipped out his multi-tool from his back pocket (never know when you're going to need one!) and started to saw at Ruby's constraints.

"Nice try, daddy-o."

Carl spun around. The man with the hat was back.

"The bomb's a dud. She's just the bait. You're coming with me."

Carl's world went black.

* * *

Carl awoke with a start. He had always prided himself on being the sort of person that could jerk himself out of sleep at a moment's notice, and here he was, proving himself right yet again. Where was he? The room was nondescript enough. It reminded Carl of the training camp segments in his war movies — a simple trunk at the foot of a simple twin bed. Unadorned walls. Itchy blankets. Carl noticed that he wasn't wearing any clothes save his trusty white briefs (what a deal he got on them!). He sat up and meandered around the room, looking for something to cover up with; it was awfully cold in there. He opened the trunk and something surprising was in there — it looked *exactly* like his softball uniform. He inspected it; it had the same logo on the front (Ned Gundersson's Farming Supply) and his number (lucky 8!) and name on the back. But then he noticed a familiar mustard stain just below the collar. How could it be? Had they been in his house? Was his family all right? What about Ruby? He slid on the familiar three-quarter-length shirt and sweatpants and strode over to the door.

Carl pressed his ear to the surface of the door and closed his eyes, listening for any activity outside. He didn't hear anything, and despite what his *kids* were always saying, his hearing was perfectly fine, thank you. Nothing outside. He pulled on the door handle and . . . it didn't budge. He sat down on the bed, defeated, and rested his head in his hands. What had happened to his life?

The door swung open with a bang. Whoever had just entered clicked the door shut and towered over the foot of his bed. Carl's head was swimming and things were coming into focus slowly. It was the man from before, now without his hat.

"Call me Mr. O," he said. His voice was still and calm, much like the waters at Big Turtle Lake, probably his favorite fishing spot (if you're up in the northern part of Minnesota, for sure).

"What's going on?" Carl asked. "Where's Ruby?"

"Safe," Mr. O said, and he gestured for Carl to get up. "She'll be fine. Just a little shell-shocked."

"Good," Carl said. "Make sure you give her one of those space blankets. She was not wearing enough to go out on a night like this."

Mr. O motioned for Carl to follow him down the hallway. "I apologize for all the subterfuge. It was necessary to get you here."

"Where are we?" asked Carl.

"An undisclosed location, Mr. Anderson. Why do you think we knocked you out?" Mr. O replied gruffly as they rounded the corner at the hallway's end. A complicated-looking door stood in their way, and Mr. O inserted a card from his front pocket into a slot on the side. He punched in a code and rested his index finger on a scanner that slid open in front of them. He then punched in another code.

"That's a lot of codes to remember!" said Carl. "I'd probably have to start writing 'em down."

Mr. O glared silently at Carl and opened the door, which made a loud hissing noise as its various locks depressurized.

They stepped into another room, but this one was different from everywhere else. It was a batting cage! The familiar netting was hung up in aisles all around them, each aisle with an area for a batter to stand and a pitching machine. A man dressed like a sergeant was standing in front of one of the pitching machines, holding a softball with a small group of uniformed men. He extended it to Carl.

"Do me a favor, Carl. Show me and Sgt. Hampton your pitch."

Carl looked down at the home plate on the other end of the aisle. Situated next to the plate was an odd-looking machine. Carl knew gadgets, but this one was totally unfamiliar to him. He wondered if it was from the Sharper Image. Carl reluctantly took the ball and tossed it down the middle, past the machine and over the plate. A screen mounted on the top of the machine flashed NEGATIVE. A few of the men around Sgt. Hampton began to whisper to one another.

"Quiet!" Hampton snapped. "Carl, how about you show us the Anderson curve, eh?"

Carl was taken aback. His famous curve? His father's famous curve? Anderson men were taught that pitch when they were old enough to wield a softball, and sure, his fame extended all over northern Cass County, but all the way here? Wherever they were? Sgt. Hampton handed Carl another softball and stepped away. The uniformed men looked at him, intently. Carl took a deep breath. He reared back and fired his curve—his famous curve—his MVP three-years-running curve—past the machine and over the plate.

Carl, the oddly uniformed men, Sgt. Hampton, Mr. O, they all looked at the machine expectantly. The screen came to life. POSITIVE.

The uniformed men looked at each other, some in apparent disbelief, others looking comforted. Carl looked over at Sgt. Hampton, who was striding over, grinning ear to ear.

"Carl, you're going to save the president."

JIM HOPPER *is the award-winning author of* The Patriarch's Puzzlement *and* The Sire's Fire. *He lives with his wife and three kids in Spokane, WA.*

Father of Danger *will be released this fall from Kirk's Books.*

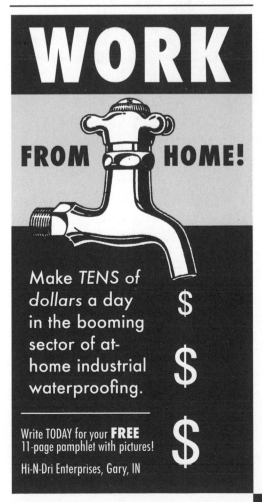

NEXT MONTH:

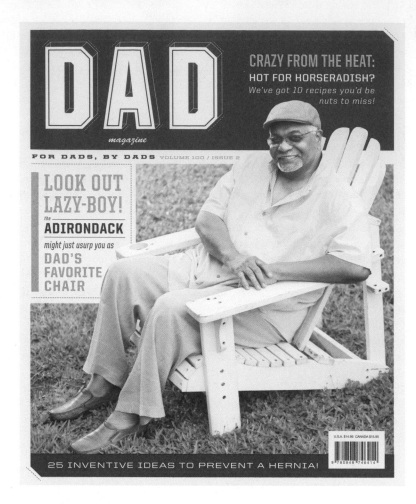

QUIZ: HOW COOL OF A DAD ARE YOU?
Wondering if your kids think you're a rad-dad or just a lame-duck? Take this revealing quiz and find out.

WHY MISPRONOUNCING WORDS IS JUST FINE, AND WHY YOUR SON SHOULD GET OFF YOUR CASE
Yes, you know "thee-ater" is really supposed to be pronounced "theater," but you've been on this earth long enough to have earned the right to pronounce it however you darn well please.

COVER STORY: MOVE OVER LAZY-BOY, THERE'S A NEW KID IN TOWN
All across the nation, the Adirondack chair is taking over as Dad's favorite place to rest his caboose (or at least while the weather's warm).

TANTALIZE YOUR TONGUE WHILE CLEARING YOUR SINUS PASSAGES:
10 scorching recipes based on your favorite condiment; horseradish!

BOOK CLUB: JERRY MCGILLS'S NEW BOOK ORAL HISTORY OF HISTORY BOOKS: A HISTORY
We've got an exclusive preview of the Pulitzer Prize winning author's riveting history of oral history.

THE WAY ATHLETES ARE ACTING; WE'RE LOOKING INTO IT
Can you believe the way today's athletes are behaving?